The Project Planning Workshop Handbook

The Project Planning Workshop Handbook

How to Plan Your Project and Motivate Your Team to Deliver it On Time

Bryan Barrow

The Project Planning Workshop Handbook

First published in 2016 by

Thembi Publishing
(a division of Nova Consulting Limited)

18 Bath Road, Swindon, Wiltshire SN1 1BA

info@nova-consulting.co.uk
www.nova-consulting.co.uk

ISBN-10 1523254092
ISBN-13 978-1523254095

A CIP catalogue entry for this book is available from the British Library.

This book is available online and at bookstores.

To everyone who ever felt
the calling to become
a project manager
- this is for you!

Table of Contents

A Crisis Just Around the Corner	13
A Comparison of Different Planning Approaches	31
Why Index Card Planning works	53
Planning your Workshop	65
What you need for your Index Card Planning workshop	79
Preparing For Your First Index Card Planning Workshop	85
Running your Index Card Planning Workshop	95
Following up after your Workshop	135
The Key Business Benefits of Facilitated Planning Workshops	143
Frequently Asked Questions	147
Conclusion	159
About The Author	163
References	167
Further Reading	169

Notice of Liability

The author and publisher have made every effort to ensure that the accuracy of the information herein. However, the information contained in this Handbook is sold without warranty, either express or implied. Neither the author or its dealers or distributors will be held liable for any damages to be caused either directly or indirectly by the instructions contained in this Book, or by the software or hardware products contained herein.

Trademark Notice

Rather than indicating every occurrence of a trademark name as such, this Handbook uses the names only in an editorial fashion and to the benefit of the trademark owner with no intention or infringement of the trademark.

Income Disclaimer

This book contains business strategies, marketing methods and other business advice that, regardless of my own results and experience, may not produce the same results (or any results) for you. I make absolutely no guarantee, expressed or implied, that by following the advice below you will make any money or improve current profits, as there are several factors and variables that come into play regarding any given business.

Primarily, results will depend on the nature of the product or business model, the conditions of the marketplace, the experience of the individual, and situations and elements that are beyond your control.

As with any business endeavor, you assume all risk related to investment and money based on your own discretion and at your own potential expense.

Liability Disclaimer

By reading this book, you assume all risks associated with using the advice given below, with a full understanding that you, solely, are responsible for anything that may occur as a result of putting this information into action in any way, and regardless of your interpretation of the advice.

You further agree that our company cannot be held responsible in any way for the success or failure of your business as a result of the information presented in this book. It is your responsibility to conduct your own due diligence regarding the safe and successful operation of your business if you intend to apply any of our information in any way to your business operations.

Foreword

About this Handbook

Welcome to the Project Planning Workshop Handbook and the **Index Card Planning Method**. Whether you're just starting out in project management, are a more experienced project professional who is looking to get better at it, or are a member of a project management office (PMO) who works with project management professionals with a wide range of skills and experience, this Handbook has the tools that you need to help you to plan projects better.

The ability to plan a project is a wonderful skill to have. It really is difficult to overstate this. You may feel that you already know how to plan a project because you have run successful projects in the past. I am not going to challenge your belief. What I *will* say is that projects are more likely to fail - to come in late, over budget, or fail to deliver the intended benefits - than they are to succeed.

If you have worked in project management for any length of time you will know this to be true. If you do not work in project management, but have the pleasure, or misfortune, to manage the occasional project then this reality may come as a shock to you. My hope is that the shock that you feel is limited to hearing about the low levels of project success that others achieve, because you learn how to deliver projects through the information contained in this Handbook. Let me say that you just need to find one thing in this Book that works for you. Take it, and make it your own and use it from here on as part of the way that you manage projects. If you do this then you will without doubt not only justify your investment, but reap a reward much more substantial.

Your Feedback

If you have any questions about any of the information contained in this Handbook, the best way to get a quick response is to email feedback@bryanbarrow.com. We especially welcome any suggestions for improvement.

Getting Started

While every effort has been made to ensure the accuracy of the information and documents herein, the author will not be held liable for any damages caused by the instructions or document contained in The Project Planning Workshop Handbook. That's the legal stuff out of the way, so let's get started!

Chapter 1

A Crisis Just Around the Corner

Whether you know it or not, we are approaching a critical time for the project management profession. If you are dependent on the successful delivery of projects in your organisation this may also be a critical time for your career too, whether you are:

- Accountable for *delivering individual projects* - a Project Manager, Delivery Manager, Operations Manager, Team Leader or Consultant;
- Accountable for *delivering multiple projects* – a Programme Manager or Project Management Office (PMO) Manager;
- Accountable for ensuring the *delivery of benefits* –Portfolio Manager, Project Director or Chief Operations Officer (COO);
- Accountable for *finding the funding* for projects – Chief Financial Officer (CFO), Divisional Finance Director;
- Accountable for the *successful execution of strategy* in your organisation - Chief Executive Officer (CEO), Managing Director (MD) or Chief Information Officer (CIO).

The importance of project management

Over the past 20 years we have seen the ongoing acceptance of project management as a vital discipline by business, to the point where there is now widespread agreement that project management is vital to business performance and organisational success.

It is difficult to overstate the need for good project management because your career is probably dependent on it. About half of the U.S. Gross Domestic Project (GDP) is delivered through projects, while here in the U.K. more than £250Bn is spent on projects each year.

Project management is vital to executing strategy, so you need people with project management skills if you are to turn strategy into reality.

Increasing demand for people with project management skills

Over the period 2011 - 2021 we can expect to see more than 15 million new jobs created in the project management industry across the globe. There is already a healthy demand for people with project management skills and, as a result, salaries for people in the project management community are significantly higher than for people in non-project roles.

Good people will continue to have multiple offers for their services and they are not afraid of moving from one project to another if someone makes them an attractive offer.

All of this should be seen as good news if you are a project manager. This is terrible news if you are trying to attract or retain people with scarce project skills in order to deliver the projects and programmes that are vital to your organisation.

The growing fight for a shrinking supply

To make matters worse the baby boomer generation, those born between 1945 and 1964 are now starting to retire in greater numbers. The first of the baby boomers began the leave the workforce in 2011. This exodus will continue rising until 2019, but will continue until 2030.

So good people are leaving the industry at the very time that there is an increase in demand. This mismatch between demand and supply is already resulting in:

- Salaries for project personnel shooting up, as businesses compete for those with key skills;
- Projects being stalled for the lack of suitable personnel to lead them, leading to failure to deliver against strategic plans, and;

- More junior people being pushed to take on projects for which they do not have the necessary skills. Leading to increased rates of projects failure.

Project management failure rates are far too high

Despite the importance of project management, and the continued investment in it, the current failure rate of project management success is still too high. According to the U.S. based Standish Group less than one projects in four is delivered on time, on or under budget and delivering the full scope as required. The remainder:

- Come in late and / or over budget;
- Are cancelled before completion, usually only after the organisation has spent much or all of the original budget;
- Are delivered late, but fail to achieve the required business objectives.

Another piece of research by the Boston Consulting Group (BCG) paints an even grimmer picture. As the size of projects (in monetary terms) rises so too does the failure rate. BCG found that while 63% of projects with a budget under $750k failed to deliver, this shot up to a failure rate $93% of projects with a budget of $1M or more.

The effects of poor project management can have a drastic impact on your organisation, including:

- Lost revenue and / or profit;
- Lost opportunities – including opportunities to enter new markets, or enter into joint ventures;
- Lost customers;
- Loss of market share;
- Damaged relationships with suppliers and partners.

Failure to execute strategy is the number one reason for executive downfall

The failure to execute on strategy ultimately leads to CEOs losing their jobs, according to Oracle. A study of their conducted in 2011 study concluded that:

- CEOs were under greater pressure to deliver than ever before;
- Failure was more likely to lead to their departure than in previous years.

And it's not just CEOs; some organisations never get over a significant project setback and some careers never recover from a failed project or programme.

So what is being done to solve the problem?

The past twenty years has seen a significant focus on improving project success rates. The actions to raise levels of performance have largely fallen into three areas:

- Development of the project management profession;
- Education and training at undergraduate and postgraduate level;
- Investment in systems and tools.

As you'll soon see, none of these approaches fix the real problem, at least not quickly enough to help you in your business.

The development of project management as a profession

More and more people are becoming members of professional bodies that ever before. Organisations like the Association for Project Management (APM), the Project Management Institute (PMI), and the International Project Management Association (IPMA) have grown over the years into a powerful force for the advancement of the project management profession:

- The APM is the largest professional body of its kind in Europe, with over 20,000 individual and 500 corporate members;
- The PMI has approximately 300 chapters all over the globe and over 700,000 members;
- Founded in 1965 the IMPA is the world's first project management association. It is a federation made up of a number of *national* member associations spanning the entire globe.

More students are studying project management at university

More and more universities are providing courses in project management at both undergraduate and postgraduate level. They are turning out newly-qualified project management specialists who then go on to enter the project management profession already equipped with the basic knowledge that they need.

However it usually takes several years for them to acquire all of the skills that they need in order to become project leaders. This is especially true of the softer skills, including negotiation, influencing and persuasion.

Increased reliance on project management tools

The market for project management software is large and is dominated by five companies:

- Oracle, who took became a leading player in the market in 2008 when they acquired the project software tool Primavera;
- Microsoft, who occupy the number one spot for desktop project management software with MS Project;
- CA Technologies, the providers of the Clarity PPM range of enterprise project management products;
- Planview, a leading provider of project management software for over two decades;
- Hewlett Packard (HP), with PPM Centre taking a 4% share of the market.

The market is also changing. There are several key drivers for this latest change, including:

- The move towards software as a service (SaaS), rather than individual licensing, which provides flexibility and optimises costs;
- The need for simultaneous access by any member of the team no matter where they work;

- Integration with document management and configuration management tools;
- Integration with online collaboration / meeting software;
- Integration with email, chat and social media tools;
- The adoption of "Agile" methods, in particular the use of Scrum in which there is no real "Project Manager" role and therefore no single person responsible for project planning.

As a result of these changes new software products are coming onto the market which is increasing the fragmentation of project management software tools. These tools may have more features, be more flexible, be easier to use and in many cases be free to use but they do not lead to an improvement in project *planning* skills. The skills come first; without these the tools are useless.

Why professionalization, education and tools won't solve the coming crisis

Unfortunately, none of the three approaches above – professionalisation, higher education and software tools – will solve your current challenge: how to deliver your current key project and programmes. At least, not in the short term.

Certification of project managers is not the only answer

The size of project management associations shows that they represent just a small fraction of the active project managers working right now. There are approximately 15 million project Managers in the U.S and Canada alone, while worldwide the size of the project management community is approaching 25 million.

Even if the leading associations grow at the same rate as the size of the project management community they will still continue to represent a small piece of a much larger puzzle.

Training often only provides a short term boost to performance, if at all

The trouble with training is that it often only acts as a *short term* boost to performance. Without the reinforcement that comes through sustained application of new skills you will only see a temporary improvement in results. Training needs time for newly-acquired skills to "stick". Worse still, the focus continues to be on what is often referred to as "hard" project management skills such as cost management, resource management. More needs to be done to develop the soft project management skills sooner. This isn't happening but this book will help you to develop your soft project management skills.

The proliferation of project management software and tools won't help either

Whether the software you use supports single users, groups or the entire enterprise, the software is only as good as the information that you put into it. This information is likely to be wrong at the start and get worse as time goes on. The real data that you need to focus on is the information that you're probably not tracking. The skills that you will develop from using this book will work irrespective of the project planning tools that you use.

Where you need to focus for success now

A key reason for poor project performance is poor planning and, in particular poor estimating. Three key factors behind poor estimating are:

1. Lack of a clear goal
2. Fragmented planning
3. Poor communication and lack of collaboration.

The lack of a clear goal

This is the failure to clarify just what the goal is, in terms that everyone who needs to be involved in the project can understand. Sometimes the project goal is wrapped up in jargon, weasel-words or management-speak. Even worse is that the link to the business benefits or strategy is missing. Not only does this means that people don't know what the project goal is, they don't know why it is important to achieve it and how their efforts contribute to overall business success.

Fragmented planning

Let's imagine for a moment that you have several teams who need to work on a new project. Each team may have its own work plan or mini-plan, but unless they all work together to ensure that any interdependencies are clearly known and communicated, they risk running into problems of coordination because activities across the teams are not aligned, constraints are unclear and progress against plans is misleading. This situation is made worse if key project activities are excluded from the initial planning. Once the need for extra work becomes clear, so too does the need for extra resources, for extra funding and for extra time.

Poor communication and lack of collaboration

Despite all the advances that we have in communications technologies over the past 30 years it might seem incredible to believe that projects suffer from poor communications. Three decades ago the humble pager or beeper was the cutting edge of mobile communication. The capability of the page was limited to a short message and a number to call back, but it was the best way to connect with people on the move. Mobile phones did exist but they were bulky, had battery life often measured in minutes and struggled to sustain a reasonable connection. Now we can communicate with anyone in the world with the phone in our pockets and not just voice calls. Text messaging, live chat, live video calling all seem so matter of fact now; these are all available to most people, often for free.

However, despite all of the apparent improvements in communications technology, the reality for many organisations it is that their people and teams fail to talk to each other. Far too many people choose to send emails to their colleagues instead of picking up the phone. This is true even when they sit right next to each other! It is now common for team members not to be based in the same location; this makes the need for good communications and collaboration even more important. Whether project team members are parts of different groups, belong to different companies, work in different countries or just work from home, they need to be able to work together if the project is to succeed.

The Index Card Planning approach

It is when these three problems combine – lack of a clear goal, fragmented planning and poor communication and collaboration – that you have the conditions where your projects are more than likely to fail. If you are to succeed you have to overcome all three and your best opportunity to do this is at the planning stage.

One way that you can boost your team's collaborative approach by organising a kick-off workshop, or kick-off meeting. By holding a kick-off meeting you create a shared vision of the project and a sense of team spirit that you can build on as the project progresses.

Unfortunately too many projects start off without first holding a kickoff workshop. Those that do often waste the opportunity because the workshop is more of a communications meeting rather than a planning workshop. That's why I developed a repeatable approach that resolves the problems associated with poor planning. I call it the Index Card Planning Method.

Not only does Index Card Planning address the shortcomings of poor planning – lack of a clear goal, fragmented planning and lack of collaboration -it also deals with one other problem which has gone unresolved for over two decades: Few people know how to organise and run a project kick-off workshop.

Three reasons why Index Card Planning works

First, Index Card Planning starts with a common vision. Before going straight into planning, Index Card Planning workshops spend time discussing the project vision so that everyone understands why the project is important and how it links to your business strategy. The creation of a shared goal means that everyone is aiming at the same target and works together to achieve it. The alignment with strategy means that the right projects get delivered.

Second, Index Card Planning builds a single, *integrated* plan. Having established a common goal the team creates an integrated plan. By planning together everyone gets a common view of what needs to be done, by whom, and by when. This means no more mis-aligned activities, overlooked tasks or lack of ownership. The process of creating a single plan throws up potential dependencies, whether between different teams or else between projects and programmes. That's a good thing because you can make plans to manage the dependencies rather than be surprised by them mid-project.

Third, Index Card Planning develops leadership potential. There's a big difference between management and leadership. Index Card Planning develops leadership potential by teaching your project managers how to:

- Understand and present the big picture and relate today's activities to the achievement of tomorrow's goals;
- Focus on developing the why before going onto the how;
- Foster teamworking by breaking down barriers and building alliances across the organisation;
- Unlock peoples' ideas and creativity, so that they learn how to solve problems for themselves;
- Get people to become accountable for success, rather than being slaves to a plan that will not work.

People who learn how to plan with Index Cards develop real leadership capability because they learn how to engage with and motivate those around them. This repeatable formula delivers consistent results and develops project leadership skills.

Benefits of Index Card Planning

The benefits of Index Card Planning start with your very first workshop and they continue right through your organisation as your people start to respond to this new, better way of planning. Here are the main benefits you can expect over the short and longer term:

Benefits to Project Managers and teams:

- Clearer objectives;
- Realistic schedules and budgets;
- Boosts project leadership skills across the organisation.

Benefits to Clients and Partners:

- Faster delivery of business benefits;
- More profitable relationships.

Benefits to Sponsors and Clients, including CEOs:

- Better alignment between projects and business strategy;
- Greater ability to execute strategy.

Benefits for Finance Managers and Directors:

- Reduction in project cost overruns;
- Improved Return on Invesent (RoI).

Benefits to the Project Management Office (PMO):

- Better resource planning and utilisation ;
- Compliance with corporate governance processes.

Benefits to other organisational stakeholders:

- Better alignment between projects and business change;
- Improved morale and teamworking.

Benefits to HR:

- Reduction in workplace related stress;
- Reduced employee turnover rates.

Chapter 2

A Comparison of Different Planning Approaches

There are a number of different ways to approach planning a project. Each of them has their strengths and weaknesses and may be ideal for a particular project or situation. Some of these are more successful than others.

What follows is a summary of several of the more popular project planning approaches. It is not meant to be a definitive description of any, rather they are included so that you can see how each one provides and supports the real objectives of planning.

Most people see the purpose of planning as the creation of a project plan. However the real purpose of planning is to prepare the project team for the project that they are about to undertake. The plan itself is just one part of this. The other benefits of planning should, and must, include:

- Ensuring that the team has sufficient information about the project to know what the target is;

- Providing a common understanding of what the project needs to deliver in order to be judged a success;
- Establishing what the likely costs of the project will be and whether the project is affordable;
- Discovering what the major risks are likely to be, so that these can be investigated and mitigated;
- Building an integrated team so that the project is not affected by inter-team disputes, rivalries or barriers;
- Defining how and when the project should be reviewed to confirm that it is on target to deliver.

The following is a brief comparison of the following planning approaches:

- Straw Man Planning;
- Planning with Sticky Notes;
- RACI Modelling;
- Direct Entry into a project planning tool;
- Kanban;
- Index Card Planning.

Straw Man Planning

This is probably the easiest to do for the experienced project manager, but it is also the most hazardous. With "Straw Man" Planning:

1. The project manager creates an initial draft view of the proposed project schedule and sends it out to relevant people for their comments;

2. The recipients of the draft schedule review the proposed schedule, mark up the plan with their suggested changes and return it to the project manager;

3. The project manager updates the schedule with the suggested changes and sends out the resulting version for further comment and agreement;

4. If there are no further comments the project manger sends out a confirmation that the schedule is agreed. If there were further amendments the project manager sends out the final version of the plan as the agreed version.

There is a long list of reasons why this is an approach that you should avoid. Here are the main ones.

Too many assumptions

One person working on their own will probably not have sufficient knowledge of all aspects of the project to know what to include and what not to include*. As a result the initial draft version of the plan contains a number of assumptions about areas of the project that the project manager does not fully understand. These assumptions may go unchallenged by the recipients and end up in the final version.

* The exception to this is smaller projects being run in a single area or department, where the project manager is also the subject matter expert.

Lack of feedback

All too often the recipients fail to provide good quality feedback. They don't correct the schedule estimates, or they don't identify additional tasks that may be required, or they don't identify dependencies or constraints. Often they don't provide feedback at all, unless the project manager specifically follows up on their initial request.

Wrong or missing recipients

The project manager may know some of the people who should comment on the draft plan, but they may miss others who really do need to be involved. The recipients don't always know who else the plan has been sent to so they don't spot the omission.

As a result it is very possible that some key information is left out of the schedule. By the time that this comes to light it may be too late and the schedule may have been signed off as approved. It may be weeks or months before any oversight is discovered. By then it is too late to change the plan without affecting the schedule or the budget.

Lack of a shared vision

Even when the project manager involves the right recipients, they may not provide them sufficient information about the project for the recipients to fully understand what the goal of the project is. This lack of a shared vision means that each recipient may see the project differently. What is needed is the same vision, the same target to aim at, so that the team are all united around a shared objective.

Lack of team formation

The Straw Man approach does nothing to create a sense of one team. As a result, each recipient sees the schedule, and the tasks that they or their area may need to perform, as a transaction: That is, an action that they need to carry out by a certain date. They do not feel part of a team that will work together to overcome obstacles and challenges. There's a huge difference.

If everything goes according to plan that won't be a problem. But, as you know, nothing goes according to plan. That is why we need teams to work together.

Rich Picture

The rich picture approach to planning grew out of a desire to get a better understanding of the total project – the background, the existing problems, what is needed and what success will mean for the organisation.

The rich picture approach brings everyone together to develop a visual representation of the project, including any details that the participants believe will have a bearing on the project.

Advantages of the Rich Picture approach

By creating a graphical representation of the project the participants can express key aspects of the project without having to put it into words. Each element of the picture adds more detail so that everyone gets a better, more comprehensive view of what the project will entail. The result is:

- A shared view of the project;
- Better utilisation of the participants' knowledge and understanding of the situation, and;

- Better buy-in from those attending.

Disadvantages of the Rich Picture approach

The downside to the rich picture is that it is just that – a picture. Rich Picture Modelling does little on its own to create the details of the plan required to deliver the project. It does not:

- Identify the major milestones or the detailed project activities;
- Clarify the key project interdependencies;
- Enforce compliance with existing standards and policies.

Overall, while Rich Picture Modelling is suitable for creating a vision of the project and for stimulating discussion about scope and the planned result of the change, it does not do enough to support detailed planning.

Planning With Sticky Notes

With sticky note planning the project team work together to create a Work Breakdown Structure for the project that covers all of the work that project needs to complete. Once completed the project manager converts the Work Breakdown Structure into a project schedule.

The Benefits of planning with sticky notes

Overall this approach does provide project leaders and teams with a sense of what needs to done to deliver the project. It is good at bringing people together to discuss the project and for identifying high level activities. Yet, this is not without disadvantages. Here's a light-hearted summary of what *can* happen to your project when you plan using sticky notes:

1. You organise the workshop a few weeks ahead of time so that the attendees have sufficient time to prepare for the event. People don't prepare for the event though. They know that it's a sticky note workshop so they can just do what they need to when they get there;

2. You brief the participants on the goal of the project and the expected outcome. At least, you do for those who bothered to turn up; some people fail to show up and others send deputies instead of going themselves;

3. Everyone writes down the key activities that they will need to complete to deliver the project. The person deputising for the subject matter expert often knows less than they should and this is reflected in the quality of their submissions.

Other subject matter experts (SMEs) may forget several things because they are reliant on memory and didn't prepare in advance;

4. After a few furious minutes spent writing and sticking notes to the wall or whiteboard everyone reads what the other participants have written. They then make changes or add more notes to the wall. Often the writing is too small, or too awful to read because of the small size of the notes and the fact that people are in a hurry to write everything down;

5. As a group you review and move the sticky notes around until you are all happy that you have thought of everything. Then the notes start falling off the wall;

6. You spend the remainder of the workshop trying to walk through the plan with notes falling off and being put back. Sometimes the notes are put back in the wrong place. Sometime they are put back upside down. Some notes keep on falling off;

7. Then the workshop ends and everyone leaves hoping that the notes will survive being rolled up and transported to a place where the information can be transcribed onto something more useful.

5 Key Drawbacks to project planning using sticky notes

Despite what I said above planning with sticky notes *can* work. It can work particularly well with smaller projects. It can also work well with Scrum and Lean projects, where there is a more formalised approach to the use of sticky notes and they are used not just for planning, but also for execution. However, as a tool for planning it has real drawbacks, including the following five:

1. **Reliance on subject matter experts.** Attendees need to be experienced in your methodology in order to successfully identify the key activities. This usually makes them hard to get hold of as they are often too busy working on projects to attend workshops. Even if they are present, you're reliant on them actively contributing to the session.

2. **Lack of consistency.** Planning workshops are usually led by project managers. Many have good facilitations kills but some do not. As a result the outcomes from current kickoff workshops range from very good to absolutely abysmal.

3. **Low levels of knowledge transfer.** The workshop can fail to take into account existing

interdependencies, re-use of knowledge, ideas and artefacts, or lessons learned from other projects. This means that projects continue to be planned in silos, leading to resource conflicts, schedule delays and missed deadlines.

4. **Lack of follow-up and follow through.** The lack of a clear and repeatable model for planning workshops means that the outcome of the event is highly variable. How often do you leave a workshop with no clear actions to take? Worse still, how often do you leave a workshop more confused by the project than when you arrived? The project may need to have several such workshops in order to create meaningful action and to get traction.

5. **Problems with facilities, layout and logistics.** This covers a range of practical considerations, including problems getting rooms big enough to hold the event in, the cost of brown paper and its lack of re-use, problems with the whole idea of planning using sticky notes in the first place, the lack of stickiness of some brands of sticky notes and the fact that every surface in the room is covered in sticky stuff!

RACI Modelling

RACI modelling aims to clarify the various participants who are involved in the production of products.

The word RACI is an acronym which stands for:

- **Responsible** – the person or team actively participates in the production of the product;
- **Accountable** – the person or team is ultimately in charge of the development of the product and in answerable for failure to deliver. There can be only one person or team accountable for any product;
- **Consulted** – the person or team must approve the product before it is finished. There must be at least one person or team consulted for each product, otherwise there is a risk that the product will not receive any effective quality assurance. At the very least the people or team accountable should perform this role, but it is better if a third party does so, otherwise there is a risk that the team creating the product fails to spot a potential problem because they are too familiar with the product;
- **Informed** – the person or team receives the finished product, but is not involved in its

approval. They usually receive the product as an input to their own work on subsequent products.

The RACI model consists of a table where:

- Each row of the table represents a participant – a person, team or organisation;
- Each column in the table represents a project product that the project will produce.

Benefits of RACI Modelling

The main benefits of RACI modelling are:

1. Clarity of role;
2. An assessment of the complexity of the project, in terms of the interdependencies;
3. It clearly separates out those who need to be involved from those who do not.

Clarity of role. One of the main benefits of RACI is a clear understanding of who needs to do what. Those named in the RACI may play one or more roles and will be involved in one way or another in at least one product. The process of going through the RACI matrix helps to clarify these roles. Each participant can see the role that they play in the project by looking across the row and seeing which of the products, represented by a column belongs to them.

The complexity of the project. Another benefit of RACI modelling is that the participants get a much better understanding just how complex the project will be in two areas: interdependencies between participants and the time needed for approvals.

Some products require not just one set of approvals but several, either because they need to be approved at several stages or else because they need to go to an approval body that requires some notice period. These can add a lot of time to a project, so clarifying these now helps to make the plan realistic.

It clearly identifies those who need to be involved from those who do not. As you go through the RACI model it becomes clear that some people who feel that they have a role in the project do not, or have only a limited and inconsequential role. In this respect, RACI modelling is useful for deciding who does not need to be involved.

Drawbacks of using RACI Modelling in a planning workshop

The downside of using RACI modelling in a planning workshop includes:

- The time taken to clarify the roles;

- The need for people with experience;
- The willingness or otherwise of people to accept accountability for their role in the project;
- Boredom!

The time taken to clarify the roles. RACI modelling isn't a quick process. First you need to agree on the products that the project will produce. This can be completed before the workshop and can be a useful way to getting people involved beforehand.

However, even when you have a list of products and, assuming that this list is correct, you still have to go through the list several times in order to correctly identify the RACI roles. It is not unusual to have more than one RACI review workshop in order to go through the entire process. As a result some avoid completing the RACI in a workshop setting, deciding instead that it is a better use of everyone's' time to do this individually. That leads to some of the same problems with Straw Man Planning.

The need for people with experience. You cannot hold a successful RACI workshop without subject matter experts who understand not just what each product is, but, more importantly, who needs to collaborate to produce them.

The willingness or otherwise of people to accept accountability for a product. Sometimes it can be easy to work out who needs to be involved in the production of a product. At other times it is not so clear. If participants are unwilling or unable to accept that they have a role in the creation of a product the workshop will be a slow and painful one. Some participants end up arguing over who should and should not be responsible for a particular product.

Sometimes the reverse is true and participants try to claim a role that they don't really have. This can be because they want to be in control of, or influence, how things get done. Although it is better to have these discussions early on, it still means that a RACI workshop can take ages and lead to a complicated plan, with too many interdependencies between people who are trying to stick their noses in where they are not needed.

Boredom! The final drawback to the RACI modelling in a project planning setting is that people get bored. The meetings are never exciting and for many the very idea of sitting there while others argue over who does what sends them to sleep. Sleepy workshop participants are the opposite of what you need at a planning workshop. You need people who are switched on, alert and active.

It gets even worse if you have to have several workshops. Once someone has sat through the first and been thoroughly bored they are less likely to want to attend the next one. As a result any follow-up workshops usually end up being done remotely or are abandoned in favour of individuals sending through their feedback. This leads us back to the same drawbacks seen in Straw Man Planning, which I won't repeat again.

Direct Entry into a Planning Tool

If RACI modelling can be difficult to do in a project workshop setting, then the direct creation of a plan with the workshop participants is even harder and the results are much worse.

The benefits of direct entry

Direct creation of a project schedule can work where the participants:

- Are knowledgeable – they are subject matter experts for the areas that they represent;
- Understand how to use the project planning software being used to create the plan, so are familiar with the presentation of the schedule on screen and can follow along without getting lost;

- Are prepared to watch someone entering information onto a tool that they themselves don't have access to.

The drawbacks of creating a plan onscreen in real time

Creating a plan directly using a tool is like:

- Taking the drawbacks of Straw Man Planning – over-reliance on a single person for much of the input, the use of assumptions, the lack of feedback, and missed products or activities, and;
- Multiplying it with the worst elements of RACI modelling – time needed to clarify roles and responsibilities, the need for subject matter experts, the need for accountability and the high likelihood of boredom.

Even if you manage to create a plan onscreen in a collaborative session there is one further downside. They may look like they are achievable, but the chances are that they just look achievable. All those pretty lines, all the neatly ordered tasks. It is just begging for someone to take one look and think that the plan is realistic.

Kanban

Projects come in all shapes and sizes, so it should not be a surprise that software to support project management should come in different shapes, sizes and presentation styles too. There is a growing trend away from tools like Microsoft Project which feature Gantt charts towards a "Kanban", or visual planning approach. Kanban tools have become more popular as a result of the growth of Lean and Six-Sigma. The visual similarity of the technique to Scrum means that more people have tried to use this for planning projects.

Benefits of a Kanban approach

Some of the claimed benefits for Kanban, namely ease of use, multi-access and visual, aren't really exclusive to that method, however the "just-in-time", visual style of planning does have its advantages because:

- It puts planning tools directly in the hands of those who will do the work;
- It is particularly good for smaller projects and those that are process-based or repetitive;
- It adapts very well to the collaborative, or outsourced model, where several people need to be kept informed of progress across the organisation or across organisations.

The drawback of Kanban in a planning setting

The main drawback of using a Kanban approach in a project setting is ensuring that the products are consistent with your organisation's methodologies; it is easy to miss something that is required because no-one remembered to include it. Another key difference is that projects are unique endeavours and they are rarely repetitive or linear. That makes it difficult to plan projects using Kanban.

Index Card Planning does overcome these limitations, so can be said to be a modified Kanban approach. This is the approach that we recommend and we'll explain why in more detail over the next few pages.

Index Card Planning

I first encountered this method a couple of years ago when I was working for a major UK bank. The bank was rolling out a new project management methodology and wanted all projects to have a kick-off workshop. As a group we discussed a number of planning approaches, including sticky notes, RACI modelling, direct creation of plans on MS Project and Kanban. Then the workshop leader suggested using cards as a substitute for sticky notes.

I saw straight away the *potential* that Index Cards offered as a way of overcoming a number of drawbacks in other methods that I had used in the past. I went away and worked on my ideas for a workshop based on Index Cards.

Two days later I held my very first workshop using this new method and it was an immediate success. Unlike most meetings these workshops were fun and high-energy. The participants loved the level of interactivity and, in particular the way that they were being asked for their views on the project, rather than being told what needed to be done; this got their full attention and involvement. Best of all they liked the fact that they left the workshop with a clear understanding of the project, their role in it and why it was important.

Pretty soon I started to receive requests from my colleagues to facilitate their kickoff workshops. I went on to use this new approach and facilitated about 30 workshops over a period of four months. Over that time I refined the method so that it became *facilitator-led* and could be repeated by the other facilitators with no loss of quality or outcome. This is the key to the success of the method and I'll explain *why* Index Card Planning works in the next chapter.

Chapter 3

Why Index Card Planning works

The beauty of Index Card Planning is that the teams all contribute to a single high level plan which includes all of their respective activities. By planning together everyone gets a common view of what needs to be done, by whom, and by when. This means no more mis-aligned activities, overlooked tasks or lack of ownership.

But why plan with Index Cards? They come in different sizes but I prefer to use plain 8 x 5 inch cards because:

- They are **large enough to write clearly in large letters** so that **the text is easier to read from a distance**. If you've ever tried to read the content of a sticky note from more than a few feet away, or over someone else's shoulder, then you'll know how important this is;
- **You can pre-print information on them** so that you **minimise the time spent writing**;

- **They come in different colours, which helps to focus on different elements of the plan** as you create it;
- They are large enough to fold in half, so **that you can place them on a table. No more falling off walls!**
- **They are cheap.** The cost of cards is much, much lower than that of sticky notes, despite the difference in size.

The key benefits of using cards

The main benefits of index cards over sticky notes are:

1. **Planning with Index cards is fast!** You can produce an initial milestone plan in a matter of minutes. From there it's possible to create a detailed plan within a few hours.

2. **Planning with Index Cards facilitates knowledge sharing.** I use the reverse of the card to describe the work product. This helps participants to understand what they are and who will produce them. Each time someone attends a workshop you get to reinforce your company's methodology until the work products become second nature.

3. **Planning with Index Cards supports collaboration.** All of the index cards are available to everyone and anyone can choose a card and use it to start planning. The act of choosing which work products are required sparks conversations between attendees. Together they agree what is needed for the project and who needs to work together.

4. **It's easier to visualise the entire project when planning with Index Cards.** By placing cards on a table it is easier to see the whole project from different angles. Participants at workshops often have new insights when they walk around the table because they get a different perspective.

5. **Planning with Index Cards supports iterative planning.** The cards are used to plan the project in layers, starting with the project goal and key workstreams, and then building up the project layer by layer. This allows the participants to understand the key elements of the project without becoming overwhelmed by the detail.

6. **Planning with Index Cards supports re-use.** The cards don't last forever, but they are reusable. The cost saving isn't the important thing though, it's the time saving that comes from not writing new notes every time, coupled with the ability to use these as teaching aids for newcomers to the organisation.

7. **Planning with Index Cards ensures compliance with company standards.** By starting off with a standard set of cards it is easy to enforce the compliance with your organisation's agreed methodology. This doesn't mean that there won't be a need for a one-off artefact, but it does stop people going off and doing their own thing and drives an improvement in consistency and quality.

So, what's the catch?

I don't think there is one. There is an up-front investment in time needed to create the cards for the workshop the first time around. Even this though is an advantage, as it maximises the time spent in the workshop planning, rather than writing notes – which is not in itself planning and wastes time. Once you have a set of index cards you can use them for as long as the cards themselves last. I've used the same set for up to five workshops before I've had to replace them. Since I have mine stored as a word document I just print some more as and when I need them

That said, the approach may not work for everyone. I've had just one or two people attend my workshops who could not get used to the idea of not using sticky notes. I've also had lots more people who've come to the workshops as fan of the sticky notes approach and left three hours later converted to using index cards.

How to Plan with Index Cards

There's a lot to go through in order to run a successful Index Card Planning workshop, but this are the essential recipes for success:

1. **Invite only those who are essential.** The aim of the workshop should be to plan the project and decide whether it is viable, it is not a general communications event. Only include those responsible for assigning resources and managing interdependencies, such as team leaders and key stakeholders.

2. **Focus on the "Why?" before working out the "How?"** The most important part of the

workshop is explaining why the project is important and how it links to the business strategy or benefits. When you have a single Vision or Goal it is easier for everyone to understand how to achieve it.

3. **Determine what success looks like.** Once everyone understands why the project is needed they have a **real focus for the planning to follow**. That focus becomes even sharper if you agree on what success – the **end-result of your project** - looks like.

4. **Create a single, integrated plan.** Having a single plan **prevents** people from thinking or **working in silos**. It also helps to **promote good team working** early on.

5. **Plan the project in stages, starting from the top down.** When you create a plan from the top down, one layer at a time the **whole team gets to understand the whole plan** without being overwhelmed by the detail.

6. **Include interdependencies and constraints.** By identifying project interdependencies and constraints at the outset, you **prevent** these from **blocking or derailing**

the project later on. This is the key to managing project resources, the number one challenge for any organization running multiple concurrent projects.

7. **If the project is not achievable, cancel it now. Sometimes the best outcome** from a planning workshop is the **realization that the project cannot be delivered**. Better to deal with this now than pay a high price later.

Much of the above applies to any planning workshop, but there are a few things that are a feature of Index Card Planning. So here is a little more information that will help you to understand how to plan with Index Cards.

Index Card Planning follows a set agenda

Index Card Planning workshops follow a set agenda. This ensures that you get the right results from the workshop. The workshop typically takes three hours.

The first hour is the most important. It is in this hour that you clarify the goal and establish the link to the business benefits or strategy. The creation of a common goal means that the subsequent planning reflects the goal you're trying to achieve. It also starts the process of collaboration.

You spend the second hour creating the framework for success – the key milestones. All too often milestones in plans relate to the fulfilment of significant *project* activities. This is different. You'll use milestones to describe deliverables that in some way contribute to the future state that your project is trying to create. That way the focus will always be on the creation of tangible value to the organisation, based on the Project Vision.

The third hour is where you agree which work products are required in order to meet the key milestones. This is where you get to reinforce the use of your project methodology. This is where you get the team to become accountable for their contribution to the project. The goal in this hour is to identify only what is needed to accomplish the project, not to throw in every last possible artefact. In this hour you will also ensure that mandatory activities are included, such as risk management, project governance reviews and financial audits. This builds in good governance at the start of the project and ensures that your team builds in enough time for it.

Index Card Planning creates a plan one step at a time, from the top downwards

- Start off with the Project Vision. Describe what success will look like and link the achievement of the project with the wider business strategy;
- Divide your project into workstreams and for each workstream identify a small number of key milestones that you can use to measure progress;
- For each milestone, identify the lower level work products or artefacts that you need to procure or produce in order to achieve each milestone;
- Once you've identified the lower level work products, group the project by phase so that you can review progress periodically and assure yourself that you are on target;
- Add in any project dependencies and constraints;
- Add in your governance review points, where you will want to demonstrate that the project is still on target to deliver and can be given further funding.

Index Card Planning uses different colours to aid understanding

The cards are colour coded to make it easy to understand the various elements of the plan:

- **Blue cards** are for **workstreams**;
- **Green cards** are for **key milestones**;
- **White cards** are for **optional work products**;
- **Pink cards** are for **mandatory work products**;
- **Yellow cards** are for **key review points**;
- **Blue cards** are also used for **the timeline** and for displaying **dependencies** and **constraints**.

Index Card Planning incorporates effective project reviews into the planning stage

The key to enforcing good project governance is to do three vital things:

1. Schedule in project reviews in from day one, so that the team knows that their work will be evaluated and so that project governance group are made to play a real role to play in directing the project and assuring its success;
2. Agree the funding required for the project, but only to release it upon the successful completion of each review
3. Know when to quit by agreeing the exit criteria for the project in advance of starting work.

Index Card Planning builds in effective reviews by:

- Making the identification of review points a **specific step in the development of the plan**;
- Building into the plan **points where funding can be reviewed** and/or provided;
- **Identifying exit criteria in advance**, so that the decision to stop or cancel the project can be made using objective criteria.

Summary

Now that you have an overview of different planning approaches, including their advantages and disadvantages, it's time to move onto planning your workshop. In the next section we'll take a closer look at the Index Card Planning Workshop approach, starting with how to prepare for your workshop.

Chapter 4

Planning your Workshop

Getting Started

The key to a successful project is creating an effective plan. The key to creating an effective plan is having the right people and making sure they know the answer to three questions:

1. Why the project is needed?
2. What is it meant to deliver?
3. When it is meant to deliver?

The problem is that all too often these three questions go unanswered. By preparing for your workshop you can make sure that you answer all three so that the project sets out to hit the right target. Here's how to plan for your workshop:

- Carry out an Initial Fact-Find;
- Get a briefing from your project sponsor;
- Agree who needs to attend;
- Agree where and when to hold the workshop;
- Meet the project manager;
- Arrange the workshop.

Carry out an Initial Fact-Find

Ask for a copy of whatever project documentation already exists and go through it to collate the following information:

- Basic project information;
- The link to the business strategy;
- Information on the required outputs of the project;
- How success will be measured.

By carrying out this fact-find you are helping to clarify the project in the mind of the sponsor and others. This will help clarify the aims and objectives of the project for everyone.

This information may be described in a single project mandate or project initiation document, or else it may be spread across several documents. Some of this information may not yet have been documented. If that is the case you can highlight this so that it can be produced and agreed.

Agree the format and attendees for the workshop with your Sponsor

Success starts with a Sponsor who is committed to the method, so you need to get them involved in the workshop early on. For most facilitated workshops it's important to design the workshop around the particular objectives of the Sponsor. Since the objective of the Index Card Planning workshop is the same each time – to bring the team together so that they understand the goal, jointly plan the project and start working together as a team – it's OK to skip this design phase as the format is the same each time. What you do need to do though is confirm who the attendees will be and agree on the Sponsor's role before and during the workshop.

Get a briefing from the Project Sponsor

It is essential that you get a briefing from your sponsor so that you can understand why this project is important to them and to fill in any gaps from the initial fact-finding. Organise a brief meeting with the Project Sponsor to get their take on why the project is important and to understand how this project links in to the overall business strategy and/or benefits.

If this is your Sponsor's first Index Card Planning workshop, take them through the Index Card Planning process, explain the outputs from each stage and relate it to the project documentation that will follow. This will help them to see how the process works.

Having gone through the format of the workshop you need to agree their role in it. They have three main jobs:

1. To motivate people to attend the workshop, so that you get all of the key people in the room;

2. To attend part of the workshop themselves so that they can explain why the project is important and to make it clear that the initiative has their backing, and;

3. To get out of the room once they have set the scene, so that the remaining attendees can get on with figuring out a solution to the problem. Let them know that it is best that they leave the participants to plan the project in their absence so that they do not feel under pressure to say what they think the sponsor wants to hear.

Agree who needs to attend the workshop

Your workshop is best suited to no more than 12-14 people, so you have to choose wisely. So, who should attend?

You're best off having the team leaders, department heads and other subject matter experts. Together they are responsible for the fate of dozens of projects and for managing resources across all of them. It is they who really determine the fate of projects, since their agreement is needed to assign people to projects, recruit additional resources when they need to and to keep resources on key projects. Often they will have subject matter expertise on the project area so their insights are particularly valuable.

Go through the list of likely attendees with your Sponsor and decide who you will need at the workshop. Choose the people or roles that have most to gain from being in the room. Let your Sponsor know that attendance should be made mandatory and get their backing to postpone the workshop if people decline the invitation. It will be the Sponsor's job to ensure good attendance.

Decide where and when to hold the workshop

Once you've decided on the attendees and got your Sponsor's commitment to the workshop, identify suitable dates, ideally based around the Sponsor's diary. Get at least three potential dates from them and get them to block them out in their diary. You'll come back to them with a confirmed date once you've had a chance to check the availability of the other attendees.

Get your Sponsor's agreement to attend the first part of the project planning workshop, so that they can meet the team charged with planning the project and deliver the sponsor's briefing. This last part is very important. By getting the Sponsor to introduce the project you will confirm that this project is worth doing and is important in the eyes of senior management.

Meet the Project Manager

This part applies only if you are not the project manager but instead are acting as a facilitator only. Your goal here is to let the Project Manager know that you are not there to manage the project, but just to help them in their work in planning the project, so that it can be managed.

1. **Tell them what you've learned so far.** Summarise the information that you've received from speaking to the Sponsor and by reading through any background information that you have. Your project manager may then fill you in on details that you weren't aware of, or give you perspectives on the project from other stakeholders.

2. **Let them know that you are there to help them.** Let them know you're there to give them as much help as you can by facilitating the workshop on their behalf, so that they can focus on their role as a subject matter expert. Also let

them know that you are there to ensure that the workshop runs according to procedure and according to time. You are not there to help them undermine the Index Card Planning approach, but to enforce it.

3. **Confirm between you who will do what.** If this is their first Index Card Workshop, or yours, you need to make clear what you are expecting to do and what you expect the project manager to do in terms of preparation, execution and follow-up. **You are there to help organize** the workshop and to facilitate it, so that you can ensure a consistent approach. **They will convert the outcome** of the workshop **into the project initiation documentation and other artefacts**. It will save them a lot of time and effort if the workshop goes well, so it is in their interests for the workshop to go well.

Book your workshop venue

Once you have three potential dates for your workshop you can go ahead and book your venue. Whether you have this on-site or not, your venue needs to fulfil the following requirements:

- **Location** - be located no more than a 20-minute journey from your offices. If you have people who are not all co-located then choose somewhere near a main railway station or easy to get to from major roads;
- **Size** - a meeting room large enough to cater for a dozen people, set out in board room format, with enough room to walk around. You don't want people crammed into a small room with scarcely enough space to breathe, let alone to swing a cat;
- **Lighting** - ideally the room should have good lighting and air conditioning, or better yet, windows that you can open to let fresh air in;
- **Projector / Screen** – has a ceiling mounted projector is ideal for two reasons. First, it means not having to move it around during the workshop. Second you can leave it on to display instructions etc. If you don't have a ceiling mounted project a desk based one will do, but you will have to remove it before the planning exercise begins and won't be able to use it during the rest of the workshop;
- **Catering** - can provide refreshments before and during the workshop. I have been to several venues that were ideal, except they couldn't provide flexible catering. It's amazing how much

difference the lack of a cup of coffee makes. Try to stay away from "make it yourself" catering for drinks; you will always find someone wanting to wander off for another cup. Instead, have it delivered early and let people know there will be timed breaks.

If you can't get a suitable room on-site you should look to a local hotel, conference centre or other venue. Although it seems back to front, you need to book your venue before you know whether the participants are all free. You may need to book more than one venue to accommodate different dates, and then cancel all but the one that best fits with most peoples' availability. This will save you the hassle of having to cancel and reschedule the workshop for lack of a suitable meeting room.

Provisionally book each potential date with your venue

You may need to provisionally book several venues. If you can, visit each venue and check the room size and layout. Not all rooms are as advertised; better to spend the time up front so that you don't regret it later.

Send out the invitations

Once you've agreed the list of participants and possible dates with the Project Sponsor and / or Project Manager, send out the invites. I always recommend that the invitations go out in the Project Sponsor's name. Best of all is if the Project Sponsor sends these out. Next best is for the Project Manager to send the invites.

If you can get the Project Sponsor to invite the participants, then make sure you give them all of the information that they need, see below.

How much notice should you give?

You should allow as much time as possible so that people have a much notice as possible. Two weeks is good, three weeks is better. If you're trying to organize a workshop less than one week in advance, you're likely to run into problems because it may be too late for some, while others who may be available on the day may be away when the invite arrives, so you won't know whether they can attend or not. You may be able to get them to rearrange their work at short notice but they won't thank you for it. Any unhappiness at being pulled off other tasks may affect the quality of the workshop.

What do you need to send out?

Give people as much information as possible so that you give them every incentive to attend. If you just send out an email booking with a meeting title and no supporting documentation you are almost begging people to turn you down.

You should include the following:

- **The proposed agenda**. Index Card Planning workshops use a set agenda, so don't ask for suggested additions to the agenda;
- **A summary of the Index Card Planning approach**, so that people know what to expect at the workshop. In particular, let them know that Index Card Planning is a step-by-step approach that works and that uses a structured agenda;
- **Background information on the project**. Send no more than a page explaining what the project is about. You really want them to learn about the project together;
- **Details of the proposed venue**. Don't assume that everyone is in the same building. Provide directions to the venue and any restrictions on parking;

- **Confirmation that you are providing refreshments**. Let them know that you'll be feeding them. It won't cost much and the benefits are far outweighed by the cost. There's only one thing worse than not feeding people at your workshop and that is not telling people that you're providing food and they bring their own.

Once you have a majority of attendees on board, confirm your booking with the venue and cancel any other provisional bookings.

What happens if people can't or won't attend?

What you need for your workshop to be successful is full attendance. Too many projects start off with key attendees missing. Don't allow this project to be one of them:

- If you have a high number of people who fail to respond to the invitation you need to alert the Project Sponsor, so that they can can take the action needd to get people to the workshop, or else to reschedule it. This is not your call to make, so don't worry.
- So that there is no doubt about this, remember that it is your job to prepare for and facilitate the

workshop. It is the Project Manager's job, and that of the Sponsor, to get people to the workshop.

Conclusion

At this stage you've completed a number of key steps:

- You've got an understanding of the project and why it is needed;
- If you are acting as a facilitator for a workshop, you've met with the Project Sponsor and / or Project Manager;
- You've agreed who needs to attend your Index Card Planning workshop, booked the venue and secured your participants.

The next stage is preparing for your workshop, which will cover:

- What you'll need for your Index Card Planning workshop;
- Creating your Index Cards;
- Preparing the room.

Chapter 5

What you need for your Index Card Planning workshop

Now that you've planned your workshop, booked the venue and invited the participants it's time to move onto preparing the workshop so that you get the most out of the session. Here are some of the key things that you'll need in order to run your workshop.

Index Cards

You will need stacks of these for each workshop that you run. You should have enough spares that you won't get caught short at a workshop. As a minimum you should have about 1,200 cards, made up of the following:

- 400 Green cards;
- 400 White cards;
- 150 Yellow cards;
- 150 Red cards;
- 100 Blue cards.

If time allows try to get a set of white cards pre-printed with the details of all work products that you use in your project methodology. Print the name of the work product on one side in capital letters and in a large font.

That way you can save the time spent writing in your workshop and ensure that everyone learns the project methodology as part of the project planning

Flip Chart Paper

You'll need about half a pad for each workshop. I usually create the agenda in advance, plus a sheet that explains how to create the plan, step by step. The rest are for capturing results as you go.

Prepare the following sheets in advance. You can do this in the days leading up to the workshop. That way you won't forget to prepare them and you won't have to create them at the last minute.

I prepare the following sheets for each workshop:

- Welcome sheet – I have this showing for attendees as they arrive so that they know that they are in the right place. It also hides the other sheets so that I can reveal information as I go;
- Today's Agenda – bullet points only, which I run through at the start of the workshop so that people know that there is an agenda and this is not a free-for-all;

- A summary of the Index Card Planning approach - I use this at the start of workshop then put it up on the wall as a reminder to the attendees;
- Blank sheets for capturing risks, issues, assumptions, dependencies, constraints and decisions - I write the keywords ("RISKS", "ISSUES", etc) at the top of each one and put these up on the wall before people arrive. That way your attendees know that you will be asking about them, so it's another thing that they can cross off their list of things that they want to get from the meeting;
- A sign-in sheet – see "name badges" below.

Blu-Tak

You won't get very far without this. Remember to use a fresh pack for each workshop. Nothing is worse than trying to re-use old, crusty bits of Blu-Tack picked off a wall because you forgot to pack some yourself.

Marker Pens

You will need a whole bunch of these, both for writing on the flip chart paper and for writing on the Index Cards themselves. Pack two types:

1. A couple of boxes of chisel-tipped permanent markers for the Index Cards, and;

2. a couple of big permanent marker pens for the flip chart paper.

Don't rely on the pens that should be in any meeting room you book. They have probably been used over and over, so you never know when they will run out. Don't expect to get all of your chisel-tipped pens back, but don't worry about it.

Name Badges and Name Plates

How often do you go to a meeting or workshop where you forget someone's name after they've been introduced to you? Yes, it's embarrassing and you know that most people try to avoid using peoples' names because they are afraid to admit that they can't remember.

Instead of worrying about people's names let's fix this problem at the outset. Ask everyone to sign in on a sheet of flipchart paper when they arrive. Get them to fill in the following:

- Their **name;**
- Their **area** or **department;**

- What they have to offer to the workshop, on a **personal** level.

Also get them to write their name, department, team or area on the name plate and on a name badge. The name badge helps people remember each others' names and put a face to a name. It also helps you as the facilitator because otherwise you'll find it difficult to remember everyone's names, especially if they start moving around the room.

Chapter 6

Preparing For Your First Index Card Planning Workshop

Organising your first Index Card Planning workshop might seem like a daunting prospect, but it doesn't have to be. The beauty of planning using Index Cards is that, after the first two or three events, everyone knows what they need to do and they tend to just get on with it. However, you have to run your first two or three sessions. Here's what you need to do to make your first workshop a successful one.

Before the day of the workshop

Here's what you need to do in order to be ready on the big day.

- Create your Index Cards;
- Send out reminders to the attendees;
- Confirm whether the workshop can go ahead or not.

Create your Index Cards

Remember to use the different colours for each type of product. Here's what I recommend:

- Pink cards for mandatory products;
- White cards for optional products;
- Green cards for milestones;
- Blue cards for workstreams and for the timeline / dependencies / constraints;
- Yellow cards for governance review points.

If you are going to use pre-printed index cards then you need to get these prepared in advance. Go through your existing project methodologies to identify the names and the descriptions of key project products. You may need to do this for several sets of products, including methods for:

- Requirements gathering;
- Project planning and assurance;
- Finance and audit;
- Software-, product- or service development;
- Testing ands quality assurance;
- Procurement and Contracting;
- Business Change;
- Training and User Education.

If you are not using pre-printed cards you just need to have enough cards available for the planning exercise, but remember that your participants will spend more time writing and less time thinking and planning, so make the effort.

Send out reminders to the attendees

It's worth sending out a reminder two days before the workshop so that you get people prepared and also avoid any no-shows on the day. Remind people that attendance at the event by them or someone from their team is mandatory. If they are unable to attend themselves they need to confirm the name of their stand-in.

Once you've confirmed that everyone who needs to be there will be, create name badges for the delegates. You could ask them to write their own name badges, but not everyone does and when they do you can guarantee that several will write their names in so small that they are hard to read. Experience has shown me that you are better off writing these out yourself. I usually create them the day before, so that I know that I have them packed and ready.

Confirm whether the workshop can go ahead or not

The purpose of holding a collaborative workshop is to get all of the right people in the room so that they can jointly plan the project. What if several key people can't be there?

If you can get a substitute, then do so. Make sure that they are fully briefed and have the authority to represent their department, team or area. It's not enough for them to turn up but refer any difficult decisions to their superiors. They have to be able to fully participate and that means having decision-making authority.

If you can't get a substitute, then reschedule the workshop for another day. If you do need to cancel the workshop do so as soon as you know so that your attendees can rearrange their travel and work plans. No-one will thank you for doing so but you will not do anyone any favours if you press on with a workshop at which key people are absent.

What if you can't reschedule the workshop and are forced to go ahead? Just remember that you won't have all of the key people that you need and that, as a result the quality of the information will be reduced.

On the day of the workshop

You've now completed the majority of the preparations, so you have very little left to do. What is left should take less than an hour from start to finish.

Confirm the domestic arrangements on arrival

Aim to arrive one hour before the planned start of the workshop. On arrival at the venue:

- Check whether there is a fire drill planned for the day so that you can advise the attendees;
- Confirm the location of fire exits relative to your meeting room;
- Confirm the timing for the delivery of any refreshments; you should have tea and coffee available when the delegates arrive, plus more refreshments to arrive half way through the workshop.

Prepare the room

You should allow about 45 minutes before the start of your workshop in order to fully prepare the room. That will give you enough time to get ready before people start arriving. It will also give you time to sort out any last minute problems with equipment, refreshments or consumables.

Check and adjust the layout. Check that the room is laid out as you need it, in board room format, and that you have sufficient chairs for all attendees. Check and adjust the room temperature and make sure that you know how to adjust the heating if you need to.

Check your consumables. Check that you have enough flip chart paper and pens. You'll have your own pens anyway but you'll need to have sufficient flip chart paper for the exercises and for capturing actions.

Remove any information from the walls that is not required. Get rid of any old flip chart paper so that there is nothing to draw peoples' attention away from your workshop. Also make sure that you have a clean whiteboard. If not, give it a quick clean.

Sometimes you'll arrive in a meeting room and find that the whiteboard is covered in writing with a sign saying: "PLEASE DO NOT REMOVE". Remove it. If it is important it probably contains sensitive information. Besides, if the authors really wanted it they should have made a copy. Get rid of it.

Power up and check any audiovisual equipment. Plug in your laptop and put your presentation on so that you have a welcome message for your delegates when they arrive. That way you'll confirm that the projector (and the remote if it is ceiling mounted) is in good working order.

Put the flip chart sheets on the wall, ready to capture information. If you prepare these in advance it will take just a few seconds to do this. You want to do this after checking the audiovisual equipment just in case you need to switch to another room. The last thing you want to do is to remove and re-hang the sheets. Now is also the time to hang up the sign-in sheet. Put this near the door so that people can sign it as they arrive.

Prepare the meeting room table. Clear everything off the table that is not needed for the workshop. If the room has a phone then move it off the meeting room table because you will need the space later.

Lay out the Name Badges and Name Plates. Set these out in front of each chair, with a chisel-tipped permanent marker pen by each one.

Now that you've got the walls decorated, have your projector on and working, and have coffee standing by, you're ready for the workshop itself. Before the workshop participants arrive take a few minutes to clear your mind so that you are relaxed and ready.

If you have ordered refreshments and they haven't arrived yet, chase this up now. If you've brought your own flasks for teas and coffees then make it now. If you're using a coffee machine then there's nothing for you to do. When your delegates arrive they will see that you're well prepared. This will help to get them in the right frame of mind.

Next Step: Running Your Workshop

By now you have a good idea of the project and of the Index Card Planning process. You have prepared the Sponsor, the Project Manager, the participants and the room. Most people don't approach a planning workshop with this level of detail, which is why their projects usually go wrong soon afterwards. You've done a great job and your preparations are about to bear fruit.

You're ready to begin. Hopefully there is fresh coffee standing by and a roomful of people ready to get going, so let's move onto running your workshop which includes:

- The Framework for the Index Card Planning Workshop;
- Your Index Card Planning Agenda;
- The first hour – agreeing the project goal;
- The second hour – creating the high level plan;
- The third hour – creating the detailed plan;
- Agreeing follow-up actions.

Chapter 7

Running your Index Card Planning Workshop

So you've identified the key participants, sent out the invitations, created your workshop materials, prepared the room and your delegates have finally arrived. How do you take them from a being a group of individuals to becoming a committed, motivated team? How do you do that time after time, with most people feeling that the session was highly valuable and looking forward to the next workshop like this? How do you do it in less than one day?

This chapter contains everything that you need to know in order to run your Index Card Planning Workshop.

How long should your Index Card Planning Workshop take and when is the best time to hold it?

A typical Index Card Planning Workshop takes 3-4 hours from start to finish, depending on whether you include lunch. If you're running your first workshop you'd be better off playing it safe and booking a four hour time slot. Once you've run several of these then you may feel more comfortable booking a shorter time slot.

If you can, hold your workshop in the morning. There are several reasons why the morning tends to work better:

1. People tend to be awake and alert first thing in the morning and, if you've sent them out a timely reminder, they will have spent the night at least subconsciously preparing;

2. Also, if you hold a workshop in the morning you can end it with lunch. This gives people the opportunity to finish the workshop with a bite to eat and a chance to start getting to know the other participants;

3. If you book an afternoon workshop you run the risk of attendees going into the office or starting work first and getting stuck on some other tasks. They are more likely to arrive late and with their minds on other things;

4. The other problem with afternoon workshops is that the day can end with people watching the clock and already thinking about going home.

As for days of the week, avoid Mondays and Fridays if you can because these are the days which are people are most likely to book so that they can a long weekend. For others it is a day that they work from home as a trade-off for travelling during the week.

The framework for an Index Card Planning Workshop

You can think of the workshop as having three, one-hour elements:

- **The first hour is for Setting the Scene**. This is the most important session of the three. It covers everything from the initial introductions to creating a vision of how things might be when the project is successfully delivered. Most important though is the rationale for completing the project, or the "why?";
- **The second hour is for High Level Planning**. This session creates the roadmap for the project's completion. It results in a plan that is sufficiently high level for the sponsors and senior stakeholders to understand it and acts as a stepping stone towards detailed planning. Once this is done the project team will have the ability to report progress against the high level plan

based on the detail taken directly from the low level plan;

- **The third hour is for Detailed Planning**. In this session the delegates create a plan which is unique to this project, but which is based on the company's approved methodologies. This plan includes the activities required for proper risk management, financial control and project governance. It also supports the development of project management skills across the organization, as this method uses the same consistent approach, artefacts and outputs. Anyone who attends one of the planning workshops will have no trouble understanding the plans of any other project across the organisation, provided that they too use the same Index Card Planning approach.

The Agenda for your Index Card Planning workshop

Here's the three hours broken down to show the specific activities for each of the three hours. Some of the agenda items are shown in bold; these are the items that I normally tell people are on the agenda, so that they know that there is a structure. I don't tell them how long each item is planned to take; that is too much detail.

1. First Hour – Setting the scene (approx. 60 mins):

    - **Welcome, Agenda** and Icebreaker Exercise (5 mins);
    - **Introductions** (10 mins);
    - **Goal of the workshop** (5 mins);
    - **Expectations** (10 mins);
    - Goal of the project (10 mins);
    - What Success Looks Like (10 mins);
    - Introduction to The Index Card Planning Exercise (5 mins).

2. Second Hour – High level planning (approx. 60 mins):

    - Dividing the project into **Major Workstreams** (5 mins);
    - Identifying **Key Milestones** (40 mins);
    - Agreeing the High Level Plan (5 mins).

3. Third Hour – Detailed planning (approx. 60 mins):

    - Create the Low Level Plan using **Optional Work Products** (25 mins);
    - Add Mandatory Work Products (5 mins);
    - Add the Timeline and Re-Shape the Low Level Plan (5 mins);

- Add **Dependencies and Constraints** (5 mins);
- Add Governance Gateway Review Points, Funding Points and Exit Points (5 mins);
- Reviewing the project's **Risks Issues, Assumptions, Dependencies, Decisions and Constraints** (5 mins);
- **Review the expectations** from the start of the workshop (5 mins);
- Check for the best insights from the workshop (5 mins).

In case you're wondering, the first item that I show on my agenda reads "Welcome, Agenda and Introductions". I skip the bit about the icebreaker so that I don't frighten those who don't like them!

The First Hour – Setting the scene

In this hour you will bring the team together, get them to understand what the project is about and why it is important and start a discussion about what the outcome of the project will be on the business. This is the most important step in the workshop. If you do this correctly you will create the environment that makes the rest of the workshop a success. You will also give everyone the same understanding of the purpose of the project and you will start the process of building commitment.

Welcome, Agenda and Icebreaker Exercise (5 mins)

Start the workshop on time and with high energy. Introduce yourself as the facilitator; tell them that you are there to facilitate a workshop for them so that it becomes easier for them to create a plan that will deliver.

Put up the Agenda slide on the projector or flipchart and explain how the session will work. Now is the right time to go through the domestic arrangements (when breaks will happen, where the comfort rooms are, whether there are any fire drills planned for the day, where the exits are, etc.). I often find that the flipchart version of the agenda works better because you can put it up on the wall immediately afterwards as a reminder.

Point out the sheets for capturing the Risks, Issues, Assumptions, Dependencies, Constraints and Decisions. Let everyone know that you aim to record items as they come up rather than at one fixed point in the workshop. Also let them know that you'll review any items captured before the end of the workshop, so that everyone has the same understanding of what has been captured and what the next steps will be in dealing with them. There are no prizes for guessing that anything that you capture here will go into:

- The initial Risk Log;
- The initial Issues Log;
- The initial Project Assumptions and Constraints;
- The Decisions Log;
- The Project Schedule.

Now immediately go into the Icebreaker exercise.

Why use Icebreakers and Energisers?

The reason for doing an icebreaker is to get the workshop participants into an energized state and to get them working as a team. Make the icebreaker quick, easy and informative. Energisers are pretty much the same but used when energy levels dip or when people need a quick change of focus to clear their heads before moving onto another topic.

You don't want to make people work hard, just get them to do something that makes them interact, share something about themselves or share some information that will make other people smile.

Some of my favourites are:

1. **Getting people to line up in order**. You can do this by age, by height, by favourite number and so on. You can then get them to switch so that they have to line up in a different order. In order to line up in order they have to talk to each other, this and the time limit creates energy and often gets people laughing.

2. **Favourite cartoon character**. This works because it gets people thinking back to when they were children. It doesn't really matter which cartoon character they choose, someone else in the room will remember the character and it will trigger happy memories in the other people in the room. You can do the same thing by asking about their favourite TV programme as a kid.

3. **Favourite sweets**. Again, this dips back into childhood and gets people talking about stuff they did when they were little.

Some people don't like energisers and won't get involved. That's a fact of life and it's not something to sweat over.

Introductions (10 mins)

Now that people are energized, get them to introduce themselves. Limit this to their name, the area that they represent and whether this is their first workshop or not. That's it. You don't need them to say anything about their hopes / dreams / aspirations / achievements. Some introductions go on for so long that by the time they are done there is no time left for the workshop. Remember, if everyone speaks for two minutes and you have 12 people, that's 30 minutes of your workshop used up; 24 minutes on the introductions themselves and another 5-6 minutes with you reminding everyone to keep their introductions brief. Ten minutes is all that you need, period!

Goal of the Workshop (5 mins)

It may sound like overkill to explain the goal of the workshop. After all, it is a planning workshop so people will expect to come up with a plan at some stage. However, it is always worth spelling out what is within the scope of the workshop and what is not, especially for those who are used to running workshops in a different way. It's also worth getting agreement on the house rules that will apply during the workshop.

Let them know that the goal of the workshop is to:

- Explain the rationale for the project; why it is a goal worth achieving;
- Get the benefit of their advice, perspective and experience;
- Create a plan for successfully delivering the project and get their commitment to delivering it.

Also let them know that the goal of the workshop is not to:

- **Conduct a lessons learned review**. If you start talking about previous projects that may have gone wrong in the past, then you will open up a discussion that can quickly turn backward-focused and negative, instead of future-focused and positive;
- **Nail down every last item in the planning exercise**. If you can create a first draft of the detailed plan then that is a significant outcome. Don't try to do too much by aiming for a final version of the plan. People will need to reflect on what they've created, they will probably need to consult with their colleagues and they may not know everything. Trying to create a final plan is madness, so don't do it!
- **Assign work to particular people**. If attendees think that they are going to walk out of

the workshop with more work to do then they may not contribute. Keep the focus on what needs to be done and not on who needs to do it. That way people are not afraid to be open, especially as they can also raise concerns about resources, dependencies and constraints during the session.

Workshop rules

While you're discussing the goals of the workshop, you'd better establish a few workshop rules. Go through the rules that you would like the attendees to observe. Also ask them whether there are any other house rules that they think should apply.

Here are the ones I recommend you use:

- **Timekeeping** – Please respect the times allotted for breaks so that we start sessions on time;
- **Phones** – Please set your phone to silent or vibrate;
- **Phone calls** - Taking phone calls during the session is not acceptable. Making calls during workshops is equally unacceptable. You can return calls during the break if it is an emergency, but remember the house rule about timekeeping;

- **Note taking** – There's no need to take notes of the session; this will be documented as we go and you'll receive the output for review within a day or so. If you do want to take a few hand-written notes then go ahead. If you want to take photos of the results of the workshop as we go then that's fine;
- **Laptops and Tablets** – Please keep your laptop or tablet in your bag, you won't need it for this workshop. In particular, please don't use your laptop to record notes as this means that you won't be focusing fully on the content of the workshop. You'll receive a summary afterwards;
- **Giving feedback** – Feedback should be short and constructive. Your feedback should be on the process, not the people in the room;
- **Focus on this project** – we're here to discuss this project, not save the world. There may be issues outside of this room that we have to deal with or be aware of, but we're not here to fix these issues. The same is true of challenges in your part of the organisation; while we need to be aware of them, our goal can't be to fix them.

Expectations of the workshop (10 mins)

Once you've been through the goal of the workshop you might feel that you've done the expectation setting. Until you have understood what the attendees were hoping to get out of session you haven't. By spending a few minutes asking people what their expectations of the workshop are:

1. You will be able to confirm those expectations that are going to be covered; this is reassuring to those who may have concerns that their interests won't be addressed, and;

2. You will be able to deal with those questions or topics that aren't going to be covered at the workshop. It may be that the item will be dealt with shortly after, using the information gathered at the workshop. It may be that these items are outside the scope of the planning workshop in its entirety.

Either way, you need to be clear before you get underway that these items won't be covered so that you stop people going off topic. Write the expectations down on a sheet of flip chart paper and put these up on the wall.

Goal and scope of the project (10 mins)

At this point you're ready to transition to talking about this project in detail. From here on everything that you discuss is focused on the project at hand. It might seem like a strange time to introduce the goal of the project now, 30 minutes into the workshop; shouldn't this come right at the outset? My view is that it is better to set the context for the workshop first, then go on to discuss the project afterwards.

Spend a few minutes discussing why the project is needed, what it aims to achieve and what the expected benefits are, in quantifiable and non-quantifiable terms. Better still, get the project's Sponsor to explain the reason for the project in their own words, as:

- They will be better at describing the background to the project and why they are personally backing it;
- Their presence at the workshop will demonstrate that this is important to the company and should be taken seriously by the group.

If your Sponsor does give this briefing make sure that they stick to time. As well as describing the rationale for the project, it is worth spelling out the project scope by asking:

- What is *in scope* for the project;
- What is *out of scope* for the project, and;
- Any areas where the *scope is unclear*.

What Success Looks Like (10 mins)

Before trying to plan the project it is worth clarifying why the project is worth doing, from the point of view of the business and what a successful outcome would look and feel like, from the point of view of the stakeholders.

The best way to encourage the participants to think about their stake in the project is by first asking:

- What success would look like in business terms – time saved, money saved, money earned, improvements in the organisation's capabilities, etc.
- What success would feel like for the users of any new products or services created;
- What success would look and feel like for the people working on the project.

The key to getting all of this information out of people while still sticking to the agenda and to the schedule is keeping things brief. I cannot emphasise this enough: you want to stop people from going on and on. Some people love to talk at workshops like this, but what you want is action. Tell them that you just want the headlines and that the details can follow and will go into your project documentation, whether it is the project charter or mandate, the project schedule, the risk management plan, etc.

Introduce the Index Card Planning Exercise (5 mins)

This part of the workshop marks the transition from talking about the project to actually planning the project. Before your participants can do so you need to explain how the Index Card Planning session works:

- Put up on the flipchart the process for developing the plan and walk them through it. I normally prepare this sheet the day before the workshop so that I can just reveal the page when I'm ready. I also put this sheet on the wall so that everyone can refer to it if they need to;
- Explain the role of the different card colours and show them an example so that they can see the information on each side of the card;
- Let them know that their goal should be to come up with a plan that is fit for purpose. It does not need to use every work product imaginable, just those that are needed.

Take a break

Once you've explained how the session will work tell them that they've earned a break. Ask everyone to put their personal effects on their chair and push the chair against the wall so that there is enough room to move around the table. Once they've done that they can have a toilet break while you prepare the table for the next session, but remind them to come back promptly so that you can start the next session on time.

While your delegates are having their comfort break take the sheets related to the project's goal and what success would look like and put them up at one end of the room. If you have a projector then you should put these sheets at the opposite end of the room to the screen.

Summary

You've just completed the most important part of the workshop:

- You've given the team a common understanding of what this project is about, why it is important and what success will look like;
- You have got them energized and focused on the goal of the project by including an icebreaker, by setting their expectations of the workshop and by

making it clear that they are responsible for the creation of the plan;

- You've created the conditions for a successful workshop by setting the agenda, explaining how the Index Card Planning Exercise will work and by aligning their expectations.

Now you can move on to creating the high level plan to get there.

The Second Hour – Creating the High Level Plan

As the facilitator you've probably done most of the hard work up until now. This marks the point where the attendees take over; your role from here on in should be to support them in discussing ideas openly and ensuring that everyone has the opportunity to participate.

You have three key roles in the next session:

1. Kicking off the session so that people understand how the Index Card Planning approach works
2. Supporting and challenging where necessary, so that the participants create a high level plan that best reflects their collective experience
3. Ensuring that the outcome of this stage is good enough to take into the final stage. If the high

level plan is wrong it will make it much more difficult to create the detailed plan later on.

Kick off the high level planning session

Once your participants, return take the two yellow cards marked “Project Start” and “Project Finish”:

- Put the “Project Finish” card at the end of the table where the project goal sheets are, so that the participants use them as targets to aim towards;
- Put the “Project Start” card at the opposite end.

Divide the project into Major Workstreams

Next, get the team to decide on the major project workstreams. Try to break the project into 3-5 themes. Each one should focus on a particular aspect of the project or be the responsibility of one group or another. The names of the workstreams may vary, depending on the type of project that you have. Examples are:

- “People”, “Systems”, “Organisation”;
- “Processes”, “Environment”, “Systems”, “Technology”;
- “Hardware”, “Software”, “Testing”, “Training”;
- “Supplier A”, “Supplier B”, “Supplier C”, etc.

You don't have more than a few minutes for this stage of the high level planning and you shouldn't need more time than this. Remember, high-tempo and high energy is the key for this workshop. Write down the name of each workstream on a blue card and arrange these workstream cards in a row just after the project start card. Use the full width of the table and spread the workstream cards out.

Identify Key Milestones (40 mins)

Now that you have your major workstreams get your team to identify suitable milestones for each one. Take your set of green cards and spread them around the table. Also place marker pens around the table. Don't give pens to the team; just put them close enough for them to get for themselves.

Ask them to review the major workstreams and for each one to come up with suitable key milestones. Each milestone should relate to a tangible result, something of value that is delivered to the business and that will survive long after the project has ended. They should not relate to project deliverables. A good way to identify the key milestones is to:

- Start at the end of the project and work backwards. It's much easier to identify milestones when you know where you want to end up. Having spent some time working out what success will look like you have already identified the end result you're aiming for;

- Try to keep the number of milestones per workstream to between five and seven. Any more than that and you risk having a very detailed high level plan, which defeats the purpose of the plan. Any fewer and you risk having a very vague high-level plan;
- Describe the milestones as a state that has been achieved using the format: <<something>> is <<completed/approved/achieved>>. If you describe the milestone like this it becomes easy to identify test criteria needed to verify completion;
- Identify milestones that denote the completion of something, rather than the start of something. That doesn't mean that there won't be times when you want to mark the start of an activity, just that these should be used sparingly;
- Let the team come up with the description of the milestone. If the team describes the milestones in words that they all understand then they are more likely to see the end plan as their own, something that they can understand and can relate to. Later on the project manager can use these

workstreams and key milestones in the project schedule. This will reinforce the message that the schedule is based on their collaborative efforts.

Get the team members to:

- Write description of the milestone in big capital letters, as large as they can;
- Write on both sides of the card. That way the milestones can be seen by everyone from any part of the room;
- Fold over one corner of the top of the card. This will stop the card from opening out flat; it will instead maintain its V-shape.

Get them to place the cards in a straight line behind the workstream card, and to place the cards roughly where it should occur between the start and the finish of the project. This means that a milestone that comes early on in the project should be close to the Project Start card, while a milestone that occurs nearer the end of the project should be near the "Project Finish" card, and so on.

It's a good idea to go through the first workstream as a group, working through the milestones from the end of the project back to the beginning. Don't try to do this for each workstream though; you won't have time to work on four or five workstreams in the time allowed. Instead, trust the team to get the work done once you've worked through an example.

Spend your time as Facilitator encouraging people who may not be taking an active part, asking clarification questions about cards where things may not be clear and checking that everyone is comfortable with the way things are proceeding. Also check that the high level milestones reflect the items that are in the scope. If something is overlooked now it will be more difficult to fix later on.

Agree the High Level Plan (5 mins)

Once the team has gone through each of the workstreams and come up with the key milestones, take them through the result. Go through each workstream, checking that the milestones are in the right place; it may be necessary to move some milestones either up or down the table so that they occur at the right time relative to other milestones in other workstreams.

If you've spent your time wisely supporting, checking and challenging the work being done then this stage may go very quickly. Walk through the whole plan for agreement. Also, give each milestone a unique identifier. This will help later on when it comes to adding dependencies. Now would be a good time to check for any risks, issues, assumptions (especially planning assumptions), dependencies, and decisions. Write these up on the appropriate sheets.

Record the results of the high level planning stage

Once the team has agreed the high level plan congratulate them on completing perhaps the toughest part of the workshop. Let them take a short comfort break and get a drink or snack if they need it. Remember to remind them to be back on time for the next session.

While they are having their break use the time to take photos and a video of the result so far. This will allow you to enter the results into your project management software tool:

- Take a few pictures of the whole table with all of the index cards laid out so far;
- Take close-up pictures of the milestone cards, as if you were aiming to make a collage. Take the pictures at an angle of about 45 degrees, so that you can see the writing on each card;
- Just to be on the safe side take a video of the result too. Sometimes you can't make out the

words on the cards from the photos, so the video is a good back-up.

Summary

Congratulate everyone on their efforts so far, because they deserve it. By creating a high level plan your delegates have made decisions both about the general approach and the specific path that they will take to reach the end result. The next session will be challenging but only in terms of time. There's a lot to get through in the next hour but you have the tools and you should now have a group of delegates that are already seeing the benefits of this approach.

The Third Hour – Creating the Detailed Plan

Create the Low Level Plan using Optional Work Products (25 mins)

This won't be the toughest part of the workshop, but it may be the toughest part for people to get their heads around. The reason is that you're going to get them to collaborate and discuss what they think is required for this project and to only select the Work Products that they feel they need in order to deliver.

This may be difficult for some to accept as they may feel more comfortable with blindly following your company's methodology in its entirety. This will be liberating for others, because they have resented the bureaucracy forced on them in the past.

Take the white index cards. Divide them into small batches and place them around the table. Spread each batch out a little so that there are cards within reach of each of the delegates.

If you are using blank cards, tell your attendees that their task is to write down the names of the Work Products that we be needed to be produced in order to achieve each of the milestones.

If you are using pre-printed cards, ask your delegates to take a card and decide whether a particular Work Product is needed for this project:

- If it *is* required, they must decide which key milestone it contributes to and place the Work Product card before the milestone card, then move onto another card;
- If it is *not* required they should put in a corner at the "Project Start" end of the table;

- Let them know that they can some of the key milestones up or down the table in order to make room as they go through adding Work Products;
- If they can't see a Work Product but they feel it should be included, then they should create a new one on a blank index card.

Whether you use pre-printed cards or not, let everyone know that there are some cards, representing *Mandatory* Work Products that they will add to the plan later on. These are cards relating to project governance activities – project planning, risk management, finance, and so on.

What to do with cards that are not required?

If a particular Work Product isn't needed for this project, get them to place it in a pile in one of the corners of the table behind the "Project Start" card. If a particular work product has already been completed, then they should place the card in the opposite corner.

What if people aren't sure what a particular Work Product is?

If you have pre-printed cards you could also print a description of the work product on the reverse side. Or you could produce a document describing what each product is. Or you could check with the relevant subject matter expert for that part of the organisation.

What to do when several Work Products could be combined into one?

You may have times when several Work Products might be better being rolled into one. That's not a problem. Ask your delegates to stack Work Products on top of each other. For example, your delegates may decide that there is no need for a separate Test Strategy and Test Plan. In that case they can stack the Test Plan card on top of the Test Strategy card, signifying that these two products will be rolled into one. In this instance the Test Strategy would be included as part of the test Plan.

What about Work Products that can be completed at the same time?

If two or more Optional Work Products are completed in parallel, then they can be placed side by side. There's no need to get this exactly right, but this will help to give everyone a view of how much work might be going on in parallel on the project.

Review the Detailed Plan

Once all of the cards have been placed either adjacent to a Key Milestone or in a one of the piles at one end of the table it's time to go through the results. Walk through the plan, workstream by workstream, calling out the names of the Work Products:

- **Look for any unnecessary milestones**. These are milestones that don't have amy Optional Work Products supporting them. Get the team to decide what else should be added to the plan, otherwise the Milestone should be removed as it appears that it isn't really needed;
- **Check all the *new* cards that have been created.** These are usually needed to cover specific Work Products that relate to this project only. Ask the person who added the card what it represents. Check that the wording on these cards is written clearly on both sides;
- **Check any cards that have been nested together to confirm that this is OK with the team**. Sometimes people disagree with the idea of nesting cards, but this is one way for smaller projects to ensure that they comply with a methodology without overloading the project with too many needless activities;
- **Go through any *unused* cards at the head of the table**. Read each one, holding the card high up in the air as you do, so that everyone gets

a chance to comment on whether the decision not to use that particular Work Product is correct. You may find that two people disagree on whether a Particular Work Product is needed. In that case the decision should go to the person whose area is most likely to be performing the work. However, it may be that this Work Product is required in order for a subsequent Work Product to be produced. Don't aim to have the debate in the room, instead make a note of this on the dependencies sheet on the wall and have the respective areas discuss this after the meeting with the Project Manager.

Add Mandatory Work Products (5 mins)

Once you've completed your review of the Optional Work Products, take out the pink Mandatory Work Product cards and spread these out around the room. Ask your delegates to place these cards where they are most likely to be required. They won't necessarily fit in any of the workstreams but that's OK.

Although these are mandatory Work Products for your organisation's methodology it is also possible that, for some reason, one or more of these is not required for this project. If that is the case the Project Manager will need to get agreement from your Sponsor to do this. Make a note of this on the "Decisions" sheet so that the Project Manager can follow up after the workshop.

Once you've completed this part of the exercise your plan isn't complete, but is well on the way to being so. Thank your delegates for their efforts so far and check whether they are happy with the plan as it is. They may need to have a break at this point, but limit it to just a few minutes. In the meantime take photos and video of the plan at this stage.

Add the Timeline and Re-Shape the Detailed Plan (5 mins)

Now here comes what can be a difficult part of your workshop. So far you've asked your delegates to identify the work needed on the project in the form of a logical plan, but you have not specifically asked them to relate this to the time available. Here's where you get to do that.

Take several blue cards and fold them lengthways. Ask for details of key dates that this project needs to hit, starting from the end of the project and working backwards. Write the details across the top of the blue cards and place them standing up on one side of the table so that these run in a line down one side of the plan.

What you're trying to do here is identify whether there are key dates that have to be achieved in order for the project to be considered successful. Don't try to work out dates for each milestone; you're not trying to force the plan to fit the time, but trying to establish whether any dates that have been identified are reasonable.

Managing expectations

One of the key challenges for any project team is dealing with unrealistic expectations from Sponsors and stakeholders. Here is where you get to assemble the information that you need in order to counter these expectations:

- If you have identified the right activities required for the project you will already get a sense of whether you have enough time to deliver;
- If you have a whole bunch of cards squeezed into a short duration then you will already see points in the project where you may need more resource or more time;
- If you have some Work Products that normally take a fixed amount of time, or have some form of lead time, then you may start to see parts of the

project that may result in delays. The team may need to decide what they can do about these.

The difficult part comes when you decide that:

1. You need more time than has been suggested, in which case you need to raise this as a key project issue, or;
2. You need to deliver the project in the time available and therefore have to adjust resources accordingly. You may be able to get additional resource to deliver it with the time you have. That will add cost, but may allow you to deliver. On the other hand you may not be able to throw additional resources at this in which case you have a risky project on your hands.

Either way, record these as assumptions, issues, risks, or a combination of all three.

Add Dependencies and Constraints (5 mins)

So far you've identified several key dates that may affect how this project is delivered. Now add details of any external dependencies and constraints.

First, go through the plan and identify any Work Products that may have any major dependencies. These are factors that will be completely outside the project's ability to control but will prevent the project from proceeding if not delivered. Add these to the "Dependencies" sheet. Also identify any key constraints that the project may have to take into account. These can include major holidays, regulatory/legal requirements, financial year end, etc.

Next, discuss any pre-existing limiting factors that the project needs to take into account and make a note of these on the "Constraints" sheet. You can also add a constraint by writing it in on a blue card and placing it on the table next to the relevant milestone or work product.

Add Governance Gateway Review Points, Funding Points and Exit Points (5 mins)

You've almost completed the planning exercise. Now it's time to build in project governance activities. Use the yellow cards to represent the points where the project should be reviewed. Get the delegates to decide where in the timeline these should take place. Next, get the delegates to insert the relevant cards representing funding points for the project. These will help to establish those points during the project when the project should:

1. Confirm that financial disciplines have been followed correctly

2. Review its financial performance to ensure that the actual costs are in line with projections and it is on track not to overspend

3. Confirm that the project's business case is still valid.

Review the completed plan and agree next steps

Thank your attendees for their efforts so far, their project plan is now complete. Before moving on, walk through the finished plan making sure that the attendees are happy with it. Once they are, let them take a short break while you take photos and video of the finished plan.

Review the Risks, Issues, Assumptions, Dependencies, Decisions and Constraints

Go through the items captured during the workshop and ask whether there are any final additions. Don't try to assign these to anyone at this point; what you want to do is encourage people to be open about these items. If you try to pin people down at this stage you risk losing their contribution, as they may be afraid that every time they open their mouths they end up with more work to do. Instead, hand these off to the project manager at the end of the workshop and confirm what action they will take.

Review expectations and close the workshop

You're almost finished. Before closing the workshop you need to:

1. Review whether the participants are happy with the outcome of the session, and;
2. Make sure that everyone is clear on what will happen next.

Review the expectations from the start of the workshop (5 mins)

Go through the expectations you recorded at the start of the project and ask the delegates whether these were met or not. If you set the expectations correctly at the start you should find that the workshop has delivered what you said it would. You should also agree what will happen with those expectations that were identified as not being within the scope of the workshop to deliver. These should be included in the follow-up actions.

Check for the best insights from the workshop (5 mins)

Ask each of the delegates for their best insight of the workshop. This is a great exercise for ending on a high note; by asking for best insights you're helping to *reinforce* positive messages and learnings. You may be surprised by what you hear; so may some of the delegates. You should also ask for more detailed feedback by email later, which you can share with the delegates.

Close the Workshop

Once you've captured the best insights it's time to close the workshop. Thank the delegates for their contribution, tell them when the output will be made available, let them know that you will send them an email with a link to a feedback form for them to complete and then wish them well on their project. Don't spend more than a few minutes on this. You want people to leave the room buzzing with energy and enthusiasm. You stand the best chance of doing that by ending the workshop quickly.

Summary

That's the formula for a half-day planning workshop that creates not just an effective plan, but harnesses the power of the team and gains their commitment to the successful delivery of the project. In just 3-4 hours you will have:

1. Taken this group of individuals and started the process of turning them into a team;
2. Helped them to explore the project in a much more rich and detailed way than they would have done had they just worked with the project manager on an individual basis, or by just using sticky notes and, most importantly;
3. Created an approach to delivering the project and a plan for its implementation. True, at this stage the plan still needs some work, but you will have done about 80% of the work by this point.

The next activity is to follow up strongly after the workshop, so that you complete the planning process and maintain the momentum that the workshop has created. That's the subject of the next chapter.

Chapter 8

Following up after your Workshop

Why You Need To Follow Up After Your Index Card Planning Workshop

So the result of days, or weeks of planning has resulted in three to four hours of activity. You've facilitated your workshop and people have left, happy and excited by what is to follow.

Three things need to happen once you've finished. First, you've got to send out a summary of the workshop. Second, you need to get feedback on the workshop. Third, you have to get the workshop outputs converted into the initial project artefacts. Ideally they all need to happen within a week of the workshop.

Why do you need to act quickly? There are three reasons:

1. You want to act before people forget the details discussed;
2. You want to help the Project Manager to convert the workshop output into project documentation in as little time as possible;

3. You want to sustain the momentum and energy that came from the workshop.

Send out the results of the workshop

Don't waste the energy and good feeling that you had at the end of the workshop. Make the most of it by sending out the results of the workshop straight away. You should send out the following:

- A slide-deck that summarises the key points, so that everyone remembers what was discussed and agreed. Don't ask for additional comments; you don't want people to try to re-write history or throw in new information that wasn't captured on the day. Instead, just ask for details of any *new* risks, issues assumptions, dependencies, constraints and decisions;
- A RACI matrix, already filled in with the roles and responsibilities for all of the work products identified at the workshop;
- An estimating template that lists all of the work products and seeks estimates for each one. You should already have enough information to start converting the results of your Index Card Planning workshop into a project schedule, but you will need to obtain estimates for each of the

tasks so that you can make your plan realistic, rather than your own view of how long things should take. Make sure to get three estimates – best case, worst case and most likely case.

Also let the attendees know that you will contact them separately for feedback on the event. You could send this at the same time as you send out the summary, but if you do it will likely be overlooked.

Get feedback from your Sponsor and from the other attendees

You should get feedback from your Sponsor and from the attendees, so that you can improve on the workshop next time. There is always room for improvement and this feedback will help to gain long-term commitment to the approach.

The first time to do that is at the end of the workshop, as part of a review of expectations. You should also ask the attendees to give you feedback on an individual level, so that they can reflect on their personal highs and lows of the session. You can ask for their individual feedback in several ways:

- You can send them an email asking for their raw, unstructured feedback in their own words;

- You can send them a form to complete, like the training evaluation sheets that you normally get at the end of a training course;
- You can create a survey using SurveyMonkey or other survey tool.

Whichever format you use, you want to get feedback about the workshop, the venue and the facilitation.

First, ask for feedback about the workshop. What you most want to know is: what is the thing that made the greatest impression on them. This information is like gold dust; if you can zoom in on the things that matter to the delegates and make it better you will have a winning formula.

Next, get feedback on the venue, including the logistics. Use it to fine-tune your preparations. Did the attendees get adequate information about the venue? Were the directions to the venue accurate? Was the room suitable for the workshop? Were the refreshments delivered on time?

Next, get feedback on the facilitation. The purpose of facilitation is to make things easier. Did the use of a facilitator help to make the workshop run smoothly? Were some people allowed to dominate the workshop?

Did the team achieve the objective of creating a plan for the project?

Present the results back to the Sponsor

It's important to debrief the project Sponsor so that they know:

- What worked and what did not work on the day;
- How to make the process even better in future;
- What concerns the team had about the project, and how those concerns are being addressed.

Should you debrief the Sponsor with the Project Manager present? You don't have to have the Project Manager at that meeting but it is better that you do. That way:

1. You can be open about the concerns that the team identified without undermining the Project Manager

2. The Project Manager can feel that you are supporting them in presenting difficult issues to the Project Sponsor, who may be under pressure to commit to an unrealistic schedule

3. The Project Sponsor gets an independent view of the project, rather than an optimistic view of the

project from a Project Manager who may be tempted to present only the good news.

Translate the workshop materials into project artefacts

Your workshop will give you the basis for much of the project's initial artefacts, including:

- A Vision of the Goal and the main Success Criteria by which the project will be measured;
- The Project Schedule;
- The Initial Risks and Issues;
- Key Project Dependencies and Constraints;
- An understanding of any Exit Criteria for the project.

Send these off to the Project Manager so that they can convert these into project artefacts. If you are the Project Manager then this is a job for you, but consider using a facilitator next time. Facilitating your own workshop can certainly work, but it can also be a recipe for failure. There's a lot to do when facilitating a project kickoff workshop; as well as managing the agenda, the attendees, the venue and logistics as the project manager you're also responsible for the outputs from the meeting. This means that you're unlikely to be able to play a full part as the subject matter expert for project management. Much better to leave the running of the workshop to someone else while you are able to spend your time getting to know the other attendees, building your relationship with them and providing advice and support to the creation of the plan.

Summary

Once you've dispatched the summary, obtained feedback on the session and got the Project Manager to convert the artefacts into tangible project documentation, your work is complete. You will have created the conditions for project success for this project and the rest is up to the Project Manager and the team. Wish them all the best and give yourself a pat on the back for a job well done!

Chapter 9

The Key Business Benefits of Facilitated Planning Workshops

If you feel confident in running a workshop yourself then you have all of the information that you need to get started. Go get yourself a batch of 8" x 5" (203 x 127mm) Index cards, a handful of marker pens, sheets of flip-chart paper and you're good to go.

If you're not feeling that confident, would like to see the approach in action first or would like to have someone come in to lead a workshop or two for you first, then I'd recommend that you use an independent facilitator.

The benefits of using an independent Facilitator

The main problems experienced in planning workshops – reliance on subject matter experts, lack of consistency, low levels of knowledge transfer and lack of consistent follow-up – are all overcome through the use of a trained facilitator. Here's how:

- Your facilitator will work with you to ensure that you have the right people at your workshop and, provided that they are there, will help to draw out their expertise and share it with the rest of the participants;

- By having a facilitator lead the workshop, your project manager becomes a participant, rather than the workshop leader. This is an invaluable aid to developing collaboration. This allows them to participate fully, to view the project objectively and listen to the opinions of others in the session in a way that they could not if they were leading;
- You can expect consistently high outputs through a repeatable planning process than means you get a credible high level plan, usually in a single session;
- You can expect a high level of knowledge transfer because it is specifically built into the workshop. Your team will leave the workshop with a better understanding of the activities and problems that they need to overcome, plus a clear vision of what they need to do on the project;
- You will get consistent follow-up after the workshop through the use of time-bound action plans and the input from your own senior management in the workshop.

What you can expect from a facilitated planning workshop

- A clear understanding of what success will look like if the project is delivered;
- A credible high level plan and key milestones for achievement;
- A better informed and motivated project team;
- The basis for reliable costings and estimates;
- Successful knowledge transfer and skills development for the whole team.

The aim of facilitation is to make things easier. Why not make things easy on your project and on yourself by getting in someone whose sole task is to help you create a credible plan by harnessing the power of your key stakeholders in a way that gets their commitment.

Chapter 10

Frequently Asked Questions

What is Index Card Planning?

Index Card Planning is an approach to planning projects that overcomes traditional planning problems of lack of a clear goal, fragmented planning and lack of consistency.

What are the benefits of Index Card Planning?

The three key benefits of an Index Card Planning Workshop are clarity, confidence and commitment. First, the workshop establishes a clear goal for the project and ensures that everyone has the same understanding of why that goal is important and what the benefits are of achieving it. Second, by producing a high level plan the team confirm the best approach to achieving the project goal, taking into account all relevant factors including dependencies and constraints. Third, by bringing the team together to work through the approach, Index Card Planning helps to kick-start the commitment of the participants to achieving the goal, because they have played their part in planning it.

Who is involved in an Index Card Planning Workshop?

There are several groups who need to be represented at an Index Card Planning workshop. First, there are subject matter experts, those with knowledge of a particular specialism – Testing, IT Operations, Business Change, etc. Second, there are those who are resource managers – team leaders, practice managers, etc. They are needed so that they can understand the impact on resources and so that they can identify the right person to work on the project. Don't forget to include the project representatives – the project manager and the sponsor.

What are the tangible results of an Index Card Planning Workshop?

There are three key results of an Index Card Planning Workshop. The first is the team planning the project understand both the goal and the importance to the business of achieving that goal, at the same time. The second is the high level plan delivering the project. This doesn't just include the workstreams and key milestones; it also builds in project governance for the project steering group and those directing the project.

The third is the identification of the artefacts or deliverables that need to be completed in order to deliver the project. This speeds up the process of task estimation so that the project can be costed quickly. These results all come from a single workshop that lasts just half a day.

What kinds of projects aren't suitable for Index Card Planning?

There aren't many projects that can't be planned using Index Card Planning. The aim of the approach is to shape a project, understand whether it is viable and, if so, produce a high level plan that all of the stakeholders can agree on and use to define the project in more detail. However, projects that follow the same specific steps each time are less likely to benefit.

What's the advantage of Index Card Planning over planning with sticky notes?

Planning with sticky notes isn't a bad approach, but it does have its disadvantages when compared to Index Card Planning. These are:

- A reliance on the information carried around in subject matter experts' heads;

- A lack of consistency because there is insufficient reference back to, and reinforcement of, project methodologies and processes;
- Low levels of knowledge transfer;
- Lack of follow-up and follow through because the outputs from these workshops are not quickly translated into project planning deliverables;
- Problems with facilities, layout and logistics, which can range from inadequate preparation which means the workshop can become a free-for-all, sticky notes falling off the walls during the workshops, having the hassle of moving the results off the walls, to the wrong kind of walls to stick notes on in the first place!

What resources do I need to run an Index Card Planning Workshop?

The three key ingredients for an Index Card Planning Workshop are 8" x 5" index cards, black marker pens and a table big enough to seat a dozen people boardroom style. The minimal requirements and low cost are key reasons why Index card Planning is so valuable.

What's the right number of attendees for an Index Card Planning Workshop?

There's no exact number, but best results come when the size of team is limited to between eight and twelve:

- *Smaller* than eight and it's likely that you don't have enough people to represent all of the areas that the project needs to cover;
- *Larger* than that and it becomes difficult for everyone to participate fully.

What preparation do I need to complete before an Index Card Planning Workshop?

Like any facilitation session, planning is the key to success. To get the best out of an Index Card Planning Workshop you should spend time discussing the project and the goal with your project Sponsor and getting their support for the workshop. If it's the first workshop being run in your organisation you'll need to prepare Index Cards to represent the artefacts from your organisation's project management methodology, software development methodology and project governance approach. Finally you'll need to decide who you need to have at the workshop for maximum value. Getting the right people in the room is half the battle.

Where does Index Card Planning come in the project life cycle?

You want to have your Index Card Planning Workshop early on, after you have a project charter but before the gathering of project and business requirements. If left for too long people start going off on their own. The result is a disjointed plan and a lack of a clear goal. Worse still, you won't have a team working together, but a set of individuals working apart

Where do I go for more information on Index Card Planning?

You can find out more at IndexCardPlanning.com. The best place to start is with the articles on Index Card Planning, but there are also other tools and templates on the resources page. Don't forget to sign up for updates as the resources page does change over time.

Where is the best place to hold an Index Card Planning Workshop?

You can hold an Index Card Planning Workshop in any meeting room that has enough space to seat 16 people comfortably. You can use a large meeting room, board room, a training room or a function room at an off-site location.

Where can I get the Index Cards from?

You can get blank Index Cards from any good stationer's store.

When is the best time to hold an Index Card Planning Workshop?

The best time to have your Index Card Planning Workshop is as soon as you have your project charter drawn up. If you're managing a multi-stage project, or want to plan using rolling waves, then have individual sessions towards the end of each stage for the start of the next stage.

When is the worst time to hold an Index Card Planning Workshop?

The worst time to hold an Index Card Planning Workshop is when your project is already underway, especially if the team members haven't been jointly briefed on the goals and benefits of the project.

How does Index Card Planning work?

Index Card Planning works by:

1. Giving those responsible for delivering projects a clear goal and an understanding of why the project is important to the business;

2. Getting them to create a high level plan and key milestones, taking into account the specific constraints that may exist at the time;

3. Boosting team working and eliminating silo thinking.

How long does an Index Card Planning Workshop take?

Index Card Planning Workshops take between three and four hours. That's it! In that short space of time you'll create a vision for your project, a high level plan for delivery, an approach that meets the challenges and constraints that your project faces and a team committed to overcoming them.

Do I need special tools and equipment to run an Index Card Planning Workshop?

Not at all. The only thing that you need is a rectangular boardroom table big enough to seat 12 people, a whole stack of index cards measuring 203 mm by 127mm (8" x 5"), black permanent marker pens and flip chart paper.

Do I need to be accredited in order to run an Index Card Planning Workshop?

If I said you needed to be accredited then I'd be lying. If you want to run an Index Card Planning Workshop then this book tells you all you need to know. It does help if you have someone to facilitate it for you. If you are planning on being the facilitator of someone else's workshop just make sure that you have the facilitation skills that are necessary to get the most out of the participants.

Can I run an Index Card Planning Workshop myself, or do I need to hire someone to run it for me?

You can run an Index Card Planning Workshop yourself, but it's not recommended. The reason for that is that it helps to have someone else facilitate your workshop for you so that you can fully participate yourself. You don't need to hire someone to run it for you though; you may be able to find someone who has the skills and experience to facilitate it for you within your organisation. Trainers, coaches and mentors often make good facilitators.

Can I hold an Index Card Planning Workshop at my offices, or do I need to have it off-site?

You can hold your session on-site or off-site; it's entirely up to you.

The benefits of having your session on-site are:

1. you don't have to worry about people failing to find the venue;
2. there is little or no travelling time, and;
3. You're more likely to get good attendance.

The disadvantages of having your session onsite are:

1. it is harder to manage interruptions, in particular there is a greater risk that one or more attendees is pulled out of the meeting, and;
2. Participants may decide not to attend the whole thing because they have other meetings to attend.

Can I run an Index Card Planning Workshop for a large programme?

Yes, we've run workshops for programmes as well as projects. Here's how to adapt Index Card Planning to suit Programme Planning:

1. Hold an Index Card Planning workshop for the *programme*. Use it to shape decide the overall programme approach, build the initial programme artefacts and confirm the overall programme business case;

2. Follow up with individual workshops for *each* of the constituent projects. Create the initial project artefacts for *each* project and use the output to validate the programme business case and schedule;
3. Refine the programme level documentation after all the project workshops have been completed;

Can I run an Index Card Planning Workshop for a small project?

Of course! Despite the difference between small projects and larger ones they both need planning and coordination. The main difference is that with larger projects you may wish to plan by stage or phase.

One approach with larger projects is to hold an initial workshop to plan the overall approach and validate the business case and then to hold follow-up workshops periodically to review and re-validate the approach.

Chapter 11

Conclusion

Congratulations, you've completed the Handbook! So now what do you do?

There's a lot in this Handbook and it may take you a while to fully feel comfortable running your workshops. However, I hope that from your very first one you become a more confident, self-assured and successful facilitator of planning workshops. You may have already received positive feedback from your colleagues on the way you run your kick-off workshops. You may have noticed that you find it easier to create plans and schedules, get the resources that you need and obtain buy-in on your projects, because people understand what it is that you're trying to achieve and they appreciate the clarity and simplicity of your plans.

Here are a few things that I recommend you do to get the most out of this Handbook:

1. **Go over each chapter and highlight the key points for future reference.** There may be points that you read but didn't take in the first time around. Mark key sections and re-read them.

2. **Hold your first workshop**. Don't let this Handbook gather dust on your shelf; it was meant to be used. Offer to facilitate a workshop for colleagues if you have the opportunity. That way, you will become familiar with the Index Card Planning Method and the supporting materials in next to no time. If there are no projects starting up imminently, try holding a dummy workshop as a training exercise.

3. **Visit my website for access to free bonuses**. There is always more good advice, information and resources out there, on planning, on facilitation, on influencing and persuading. Read an article or two. Join a webinar. Sign up for email newsletters on this topic. Everything helps.

4. **Keep experimenting!** Not every workshop will go as planned. Sometimes you will need to cancel at short notice. Other time you will get a group of participants who just don't gel as a team and the planning exercise doesn't seem to work as well. Don't take it personally, sometimes these things just happen. Just don't give up on yourself or on the Index Card Planning Method; it was designed to make your life easier and to make your projects more successful. Perseverance is the key.

I hope you've enjoyed using this Handbook. If you have I would be really grateful if you'd leave me some positive feedback at feedback@bryanbarrow.com.

Review this book on Amazon

If this book has helped you in any way I'd like to ask you a small favour in return. Please take a moment to leave a positive rating for this book with Amazon so that others will be able to benefit from it as well.

Join the Index Card Planning Community

This is a critical time for the development of project management and we need desperately to get more people involved in planning projects better. That's why I've set up the Index Card Planning Group on LinkedIn. That's the place to get advice, share ideas and lessons learned, help your fellow Index Card Planners, or just have a chat. I look to seeing you there.

Wishing you success with your projects and your career,

Bryan Barrow
August 2016
http://bryanbarrow.com
info@bryanbarrow.com

162

About The Author

Bryan Barrow

International Speaker and Author

Project Leadership Expert

Bryan is the founder of Nova Consulting Limited and the inventor of the Index Card Planning method. Bryan is an entertaining speaker, facilitator and conference host, with an energetic, confident style. A member of the Professional Speaking Association of the UK and Ireland (PSA UKI), Bryan is a highly sought-after speaker to executive audiences; he also develops and presents workshops and training programmes for business leaders. He has spoken to thousands of people in many countries around the world.

Bryan's talks are packed with amusing anecdotes that stimulate and educate audiences. Bryan gives honest, straightforward advice in a no-fluff style, backed up by research, observation and results. Bryan presents information in a powerful, positive way that energises audiences so that they leave motivated, invigorated and eager to put his ideas into action.

In addition to speaking, Bryan also maintains a small list of private consultancy clients who use his services to plan and initiate new projects and programmes and to coach and mentor their project management communities.

Bryan started his solo business career in 1996 with the foundation of Nova Consulting Limited. His extensive experience includes Project Management Consultancy, Coaching and Personal Development, Event Management, Web Development, Marketing and Media.

Bryan lives in the county of Wiltshire, England, and travels throughout the UK and internationally, speaking at events and conferences and working as a conference host and session moderator.

BryanBarrow.com hosts Bryan's website for people who want to achieve greater success in their business or personal life. Bryan's range of resources includes handbooks, self-study courses, books, tips sheets and iPhone applications.

Visit http://bryanbarrow.com/products/ for more information on Bryan's keynotes, seminars, workshops, books, newsletters, articles and on-line learning environments.

Bring Bryan into your organisation

From a one-hour keynote workshop to a three-day seminar, Bryan is an authority on Project Leadership and can tailor his material to meet your specific requirements. Bryan specialises in the areas of:

- Project Planning and Mobilisation;
- Risk Management;
- Developing Project Leadership Skills;
- Communications Skills for Project Managers;
- Improving Teamwork and Collaboration.

To make contact with Bryan or to learn more about his Project Leadership Success Programme:

- Visit Bryan's website: http://bryanbarrow.com/
- Email Bryan directly: bryan@bryanbarrow.com
- Follow Bryan on Twitter: @bryanbarrow

We look forward to working with you

References

1. PcW (2013): Third Global Survey on the Current State of Project Management
2. Standish Group (1994-2012): CHAOS Report results
3. Boston Consulting Group (BCG Perspectives, 2015): 'Large-Scale IT Projects: From Nightmare to Value Creation'
4. Project Management Institute (2015): PMI's Pulse of the Profession 2015

Further Reading

The field of Project Management is an absolutely huge one and you could spend almost all of your time reading up on the subject. The books listed below are the ones that I have bought, read and recommend to others.

Not all of these books are on project management and that's a good thing. For too long the focus has been on hard project management skills, however the real successes come from the recognition that the software project management skills are what make the difference. That's why I have included some of my favourite books on communications, on self-leadership and on personal growth.

- The Project Management Institute (PMI), **'The Project Management Body of Knowledge, 5th edition'** (Project Management Institute, Inc. 2013)
- The Association for Project Management (APM), **'Planning, Scheduling, Monitoring and Control: The practical Project Management of Time, Cost and Risk'** (APM, 2015)
- S Coleman and D MacNicol, **'Project Leadership'** (Gower Publishing Limited, 2015)

- JT Brown, **'The Handbook of Program Management'** (McGraw Hill, 2008)
- S McConnell' **'The Software Project Survival Guide'** (Microsoft Press 1998)
- K Beck, '**Extreme Programming Explained'** (Addison-Wesley, 2000)
- K Beck, **'Test-Driven Development'** (Addison Wesley, 2003)
- M Gibbins-Klein, **'The Thoughtful Leader'** (Paloma Press, 2015)
- J Marsden, **'Keep Stepping!'** (Stepping Books, 2015)
- J Weissman, **'Presenting to Win: The Art of Telling Your Story'** (Pearson FT Press, 2008)
- G Davies, **'The Presentation Coach'** (Capstone Press, 2010)
- E Tolle, **'The Power of Now'** (Yellow Kite Books, 2001)

27504866R00096

Printed in Great Britain
by Amazon